Interpretation:
The Poetry
of Meaning

Interpretation:
The Poetry
of Meaning

✳

Edited by
Stanley Romaine Hopper
and David L. Miller

AN ORIGINAL HARBINGER BOOK

Harcourt, Brace & World, Inc.
NEW YORK

The editors and the publisher wish to thank the following for permission to use quotations from the books listed: Oxford University Press for the lines on page x from the Christopher Fry translation of Jean Giraudoux's *Tiger at the Gates;* Random House, Inc., for the lines on page xvi from W. H. Auden's poem "The Labyrinth," in *The Collected Poetry of W. H. Auden;* Alfred A. Knopf, Inc., for Wallace Stevens' poem "Anecdote of the Jar" on page xvii, from *The Collected Poems of Wallace Stevens;* and W. W. Norton & Company, Inc., for the lines on pages xx and xxi from the M. D. Herter Norton translation of Rainer Maria Rilke's *Sonnets to Orpheus.*

ACKNOWLEDGMENTS

THIS VOLUME OF essays is the result of The Third Consultation on Hermeneutics convened at Drew University in Madison, New Jersey, during April, 1966, under the title, "Metaphor, Symbol, Image, and Meaning." With the exception of the chapter by Norman O. Brown, the contributions were the major addresses at that interdisciplinary meeting. Professor Brown, whose keynote address at the consultation has been published as a part of his recent book, *Love's Body*,[1] kindly contributed a previous essay apropos the consultation theme to complete the scope of the present volume.

The 1966 consultation succeeded in large measure due to the joint efforts of the faculty and student body of The Graduate School of Drew University. This volume, like that consultation, reflects the work of many persons. Therefore, the editors wish to express gratitude for the help they have received: to Professor Howard C. Kee, for his assistance in publication; to Professor Karlfried Froelich, Mr. James Hollis, Mr. Carl Ridd, Mr. Lewis Archer, and Mr. Ned Wilson, for assembling the bibliography; to Mr. Gunther Rebing of Würzburg, Germany, for his translation of Beda Allemann's essay; to Mr. Robert Dell, for his translation of Heinrich Ott's essay; to Dr. Armin Paul Frank of New Haven, Connecticut, for his assistance with the bibliography on Kenneth Burke; to Mrs. Marilyn Haney and her staff, for typing the manuscript; to Mrs. Marjorie Slater, for secretarial assistance; and to the Arlo Ayres Brown Lectureship bequest, for making possible the consultation.

[1] New York: Random House, Inc., 1966.

Contents

Stanley Romaine Hopper:
Introduction

TO INVITE A READER to step across a threshold into a realm of thinking
and experiencing that may mean a radical revision of his outlook on
himself and his world is more than a little hazardous. Yet nothing
less than this is at stake in these pages. When taken singly, the essays
in this volume are forthright and explicit; when taken together they
interfuse their patterns surprisingly, like colored spokes on a revolv-
ing wheel. They carry the reader forward into unanticipated out-
comes, thus disclosing an unidentified axis, a hub of ultimacy on
which these explorations turn. This center will come clear, not on
first reading, perhaps, but when the essays are read over and pon-
dered in terms of the implicit questions asked and the constructive
suggestions ventured.

For what begins as a series of speeches from a Consultation ends
as a disclosure and a new beginning for the revision of our familiar
consciousness.

I. THE SETTING OF THE PROBLEM

Implicit in these remarks, of course, is the concession that we have
been experiencing for some decades now the breaking up of the
conceptual mirror in which, for two milleniums or more, the
Western consciousness has grown accustomed to seeing itself. The
psychical discomforts and social traumas that accompany radical
change are by this time evident. From politics to philosophy, from
science to the arts, from world upheaval to religion—everything
bears witness to it. Our classical world-picture, together with its
conceptual mirror, has shattered. In his *Tiger at the Gates*, Giraudoux put it bluntly:

HELEN: If you break the mirror, will what is reflected in it cease
to exist?

HECTOR: That is the whole question.[1]

It is not, perhaps, the whole question, but it is the first and necessary
one: and it is the question underneath the questions at issue in these
pages.

In projecting this Consultation, however, we have wished to
put the question differently. The negative features of this breakup
have been rehearsed now many times, particularly in our literature
and in our arts, where the imagination can lay hold of our distresses
obliquely and achieve through fictive candor what the culture's
collective psyche may not yet be able to tolerate. Theology
and philosophy, more deeply inured in the thought forms of the
tradition, and hedged in by protective sophistication, do not give,
as the poem may, "a candid kind to everything."[2] Philosophy (by
way of positivism, pragmatism, existentialism, phenomenology, linguistic analysis, and the questions of symbolic form) has been
moving through a radical revision of its methods and its aims.
Despite what has always seemed to me the charismatic dead weight
of the scholastic, supranaturalistic literalism of language and method
in the early work and influence of Barth, theology, too, has been
edging its way into what Auerbach has called "figural interpretation," in which "history," "event," the "Word," and the like, are
permitted to *function* symbolically, thus retaining within their
figural complex the meanings their propositional formulations have
lost. It is this development that, at bottom, has made for the
enormous and crucial importance of hermeneutics in current theological discussion, superseding the debates concerning myth and
kerygma. The problem of interpretation is prior, just as the questions it raises are more radical and more basic.[3] The radical ambiguity of much contemporary theology resides in the attempt to
retain within figural interpretation the literalistic reminiscences of
the unbroken conceptual mirror. Nevertheless, with the letting
go of the classical conceptual mirror, contemporary theology has
boldly raised the question as to whether what was reflected in it
will cease to exist—including theology itself.[4] Indeed, it might
appear (in propositional terms) that what was reflected in it is
already lost, and that theology, along with traditional linguistic
modes and presuppositions, is no longer possible. This may mean
simply that theology, in its classical modes, has explored the full
arc of its tautological possibilities, and in its latter day adjustments,

where these are less than radical, it only repeats or linguistically reinstates its emptied and exhausted forms, becoming thus the clownish cliché of itself. "A picture held us captive," wrote Wittgenstein. "And we could not get outside it, for it lay in our language and language seemed to repeat it to us inexorably." [5]

A more charitable view, however, and perhaps a more accurate one, must concede to theology itself a courageous confrontation of its own dilemma, and a persistent probing, by way of post-Barthian revisions, into the deeper questions of its message and its meaning. I should not venture to review this history in a few brief paragraphs, for it obviously demands analyses in depth of the work of Barth, Brunner, Gogarten, Bultmann, Fuchs, Ebeling, and others, together with some account of the American response to these somewhat intricate and Protean developments.

It may be useful to note, however, one quick attempt to "place" these voices in the current theological scene. It was proposed by my distinguished colleague, the late Professor Carl Michalson,[6] that the several positions of Europe's celebrated theologians were clearly exposed by the "turn" (sometimes called "reversal") in the thought of Martin Heidegger. The emergence of the "later Heidegger" (as contrasted with the "earlier Heidegger") *placed* almost automatically the persons in the drama of European religious thinking. Barth "lay to the right and Bultmann to the left," with Otto Weber and Hermann Diem still further to the right of Barth, and Ernst Fuchs and Gerhard Ebeling to the left of Bultmann; but the important thing, Michalson argued, was not that these positions were suddenly exposed, but that "a corridor (was disclosed) between them." There was, in short, a third possibility, perceived by Heinrich Ott of Basel, who proposed the doing of theology on the basis of the work of the later Heidegger.[7]

This proposal has represented for theology a challenge of central significance. It permits Ott to say, "Theology is really hermeneutic . . ." [8] Professor Michalson characterizes Ott's view more sharply: it is "systematic theology as the hermeneutical analysis of being"; while that of Bultmann (building on the work of the "early Heidegger" is "hermeneutic as the analysis of human existence." [9] Barth's theology is a theology based upon "the *being* of God," a phrase obviously in need of considerable "unpacking." These classifications permitted Professor Michalson to align himself with Barth and the Bultmann–early Heidegger–Ebeling line as against the later Heidegger-Ott line and to oppose the "historical" to the "ontological": "ontological hermeneutic is unsuited to a radically historical faith;

. . . in theology the question of the historical form of God's word will be given priority over the question of its being." [10] But then, that is just the question that is at issue here: are we not already speaking metaphorically when terms such as "historical *form*" and "God's *word*" are employed, and are we not already speaking mythologically or poetically in order, hopefully, to disclose an unveiling of (God's) being? Otherwise, are we not still thinking scholastically, literalistically, or metaphysically, and throwing ourselves open to the suspicion of latent fideism?

It was for the purpose of getting at such questions as these that the First Consultation in Hermeneutics at Drew University (1962) focused upon the hermeneutical question as such, following the Bultmann side of the issue. Both Gerhard Ebeling and Ernst Fuchs were participants in that Consultation.[11] It was then felt that the Second Consultation (1964) should follow up the later Heidegger-Ott perspective. Professor Ott and Fritz Buri of Basel participated. In both Consultations an attempt was made to relate these issues to the American discussion. Since the debate pressed more and more firmly upon the question of language and meaning it was decided that the Third Consultation (1966) should address itself to this question, but from several points of view: the philosophical, the religious (retaining continuity with the discussions preceding), and the literary. Three perspectives were seen to emerge from these discussions, and all three are in play in the essays that follow:

1. The question of religious meaning and interpretation, raised from the side of theology as hermeneutic.

2. The relevance and implications of the work of the "later Heidegger" with its appeal to poetry and the art work as the model for the thinking and saying of primary truth.

3. The place of metaphor (and symbol, image, myth, etc.) in the thinking and saying of primary truth: the metaphorical character, that is, of our language about truth and the gods.

II. THE RELEVANCE OF HEIDEGGER

It has always seemed to me that the almost imperious presence of Heidegger can best be grasped by seeing, as he sees, that "we come too late for gods and too early for Being." [12] Our times experience the "lack" or absence of God. The term "God" can no longer be translated into any actual experience of our daily lives. This is what Nietzsche meant by his formula, repeated so stridently in these days, that "God is dead." This is to be taken metaphorically. It meant for Nietzsche the decline of official Christianity as built up against the background of Platonic idealism and the tradition of Western metaphysics. Heidegger concurs, being persuaded that Western metaphysics is bankrupt and has come to its end. Metaphysics became, through Plato and Aristotle, idealistic and substantive, concerned with the question of reality; thinking became propositional, its *logos* logical, its criterion the *adequatio rei ad intellectum*. Hence the Western consciousness committed its "forgetfulness" of being. Truth became a function of a subjectivized and intellectualized mode of "knowing," placing the subject intellectualistically over against the object (whether in Plato or Descartes), and (even in Plato) truth became a question of the "correctness" of one's views. We were thus led by inadvertence into the supposition that truth is at our disposal: we stand over against it, confer value upon it, and manipulate it technically. Its Aristotelian grammar lay in our language, and our language has repeated it to us inexorably. Poetry, by the same token, became an adornment accompanying existence, just as (for Aristotle) metaphor remained an ornament upon the trees of propositional discourse. Theology too, speaking itself through this metaphysical stance, became a theo-*logic*, propositionally intact but unable to evoke the god or to let the truth be unconcealed.

Suddenly today, the "lack of God helps," as the poet Hölderlin saw. The failure of our formulae releases us unexpectedly from their tyranny: we are again in a position to retrieve Being. Theologically this is awkward. Gerhard Ebeling has noted that "a doctrine of God is today abstract speculation if the phenomenon of modern atheism is not present in it from the very beginning." [13] And again, in speaking of Heidegger's thought, he insists that theology must speak of God nonmetaphysically, which "means, according to the dominant theological tradition, godlessly." [14] Philosophically it is necessary, in Heidegger's view, to prepare an overcoming of metaphysics, so understood; and, theologically, he has remarked that "the door remains open for a nonmetaphysical God." [15] We must abide, therefore, within the "lack" of God's presence, and emulate the poet: "without fear of the appearance of godlessness he must remain near the failure ('lack') of the god, and wait long enough in the prepared proximity of the failure, until out of the proximity of the failing god the initial word is granted, which names the High One." [16]

It is the merit of Heinrich Ott to have proposed an understanding of systematic theology that would correspond to the Heideggerian perspective of thinking and speaking. This means a translation of theological discourse from the classical grammar of Western metaphysics to a mode of speaking and thinking that is commensurate with the poet's response to primary being (Heidegger's "fundamental ontology"). Truth is no longer to be found in the agreement of the intellect with the subject matter, but is to be understood in terms of the Greek notion of *a-letheia*, an unveiling or unconcealing, an occurrence. Such truth must be experienced. It is "the essential act of man": it is an encounter; it is a response. It overcomes the objectivizing characteristic of our subjectivist-objectivist style of thinking.

Two questions emerge. The first, and immediate one, is the question as to whether there can be a nonobjectivizing thinking about Being, or about God. This was the theme of the Second Consultation. The second question is the question as to what kind of language, or thinking, is appropriate to a fundamental ontology, to a language that does not commit objectification, or reification, upon its subject matter in the very mode of its utterance. This second question lies behind the theme of the essays here.

Heidegger's interest in these two consultations, when it developed that he could not be in attendance, was expressed by a series of "suggestions" addressed to the consultation on the problem of a nonobjectifying thinking and speaking in contemporary theology. There were, he thought, three themes which needed to be thought through. First, it is essential to determine *what* theology as a mode of thinking and speaking has to discuss. "That '*what*' is the Christian faith and what is believed." Second, it is necessary to determine what is meant by *objectifying* thinking and speaking *prior* to a discussion of nonobjectifying thinking and speaking. Is *all* thinking already objectifying, or is it not? If not, then it is necessary, third, to consider to what extent the problem of a nonobjectifying thinking and speaking is a genuine problem at all, or whether, indeed, something is here inquired after, the interrogation of which only thinks past the subject matter, distracts from the theme of theology and unnecessarily complicates it. What is important is that theology should understand its task: namely, to speak in accordance with its subject matter "out of faith for faith." It "becomes clear that thinking and speaking are not exhausted in theoretical-scientific representation (*Vorstellen*) and assertion. Thinking in every instance is a letting-be-said of that which shows itself, and is accordingly a cor-responding (*Entsprechen*, saying) to that which shows itself . . ."

It will be conceded that there is a place and function for

"thought" of the objectifying or scientific kind, that there is a certain objectivization implicit in every use of words; but it does not follow that all speech must reify its subject or that language may not perform an entirely different function, namely, that of bringing Being to appearance, of letting that which is appear *as* that which it is. But what is the nature of the language that brings Being to appearance?

III. THE PRIMACY OF METAPHOR

"Everything is only a metaphor; there is only poetry," according to Norman O. Brown.[17] This implies that from the propositional and "metaphysical" point of view, the nature of reality is intrinsically hidden. Within the limits of our finite perceiving it must be "grasped" in perspectival and contextual modes—that is to say mythically, metaphorically, symbolically. Even the formal analytical "system" is a representation, a symbolic net thrown upon the stars. There is always "Something More" beyond the formal inclusions of our closely threaded premises. Nevertheless we say of God, the symbol for that ungrasped Ultimacy, that "God speaks," "God acts"; or we say with Heraclitus that "the Lord whose oracle is at Delphi neither speaks nor conceals, but gives signs." These signs are the ciphers that we read, whether religiously with Pascal, or philosophically with Karl Jaspers. The reading is in either case "poetic"—"Poetry is quick as tigers, clever as cats, vivid as oranges" [18]—and we discover that it is through our imaginative grasp that we *form*-ulate our significant worlds. Heidegger found the adequate expression for this recognition in the lines from Hölderlin:

> . . . . *dichterisch wohnet*
> *Der Mensch auf dieser Erde.*[19]

Poetically man dwells upon the earth! These words were chosen as the epigraph and implicit theme of the Third Consultation. Poetry, for Heidegger, is the fundamental naming of the gods; but it is the gods themselves who bring us to language. It is through this fundamental reciprocity that the essence of language is disclosed, as well as the fact that "the foundation of human existence is conversation." [20]

From one point of view it may be urged that this is nothing more nor less than the famous *hermeneutical circle* described by Dilthey, in which every part of a literary work requires the whole to make it intelligible; yet the whole by which we manage the interpretation of the parts must itself be built up by careful scrutiny of the parts. Heidegger acknowledges this: "As the disclosedness of the 'there,' understanding always pertains to the whole of Being-in-the-world. In every understanding of the world, existence is understood with it, and *vice versa* . . ." This implies a pugnacious paradox: "Any interpretation which is to contribute understanding, must already have understood what is to be interpreted." [21] But it is not necessary to regard this logical circularity as a *vicious* circle. "What is decisive is not to get out of the circle but to come into it in the right way" . . . for "in the circle is hidden a positive possibility of the most primordial kind of knowing." [22] The dimension of understanding that is hidden here is much like the "Unconscious" in the verses of the poet:

> The centre that I cannot find
> Is known to my Unconscious Mind;
> I have no reason to despair
> Because I am already there.[23]

The truth that is already there, but that must be unconcealed, is structurally rooted "in the existential constitution of Dasein—that is, in the understanding which interprets. An entity for which, as Being-in-the-world, its Being is itself an issue, has, ontologically, a circular structure." [24] What is needed, then, is some insight into the strategies of uncovering that which already lies within the information and data that are ready to hand. It is one thing, Heidegger says, to "give a report" in which we talk about things, but it is quite another to "grasp entities in their *Being*." "For the latter task we lack not only most of the words but, above all, the 'grammar.' " [25]

Three clues to such a "grammar" may be specified in Heidegger's work.

The first has to do with what he terms the *as*-structure of our seeing. It is the *as* factor that makes up the structure of explicitness of anything that is "understood." The structure is implicit in our seeing, even when suppressed, passed over or "ontically unexpressed." Which means that our understanding-seeing is essentially metaphorical, whether the metaphorical likeness (the acknowledged *as* structure) is recognized or unexpressed. But "if the 'as' is ontically unexpressed, this must not seduce us into overlooking it as *a constitutive state for understanding, existential* and *a priori*." [26]

The second has to do with his analysis of the term "truth," signifying that which shows itself. It is the *logos as a-letheia*, an understanding that is pre-Socratic, going back at least at far as

Heraclitus. As Julián Marías points out in his essay, this is a concept of truth that is itself metaphorical. To define "truth" conceptually in theoretical ways is precisely, for Heidegger, to cover up the meaning that early Greek thought gave to it.

Both of these clues to meaning are developed in the early Heidegger, but it is not difficult to move to the third clue, which belongs to the later period of his work, namely, his bringing forward of the poem and the art work as the model for that kind of unconcealing of Being that is central to this Consultation's discussion. The basis for it is certainly laid already in *Being and Time* in his definition of phenomenology. It means, he says, "to let that which shows itself be seen from itself in the very way in which it shows itself from itself." [27] It is through the art work that we are enabled to see what a thing is as it is in itself. The art work "assembles" things into "world."

This can be illustrated quite simply by way of a poem of Wallace Stevens, which he calls "Anecdote of the Jar":

> I placed a jar in Tennessee,
> And round it was, upon a hill.
> It made the slovenly wilderness
> Surround that hill.
>
> The wilderness rose up to it,
> And sprawled around, no longer wild.
> The jar was round upon the ground
> And tall and of a port in air.
>
> It took dominion everywhere.
> The jar was gray and bare.
> It did not give of bird or bush,
> Like nothing else in Tennessee.[28]

This is, quite simply, the anecdote of the art work. The placing of the art work in the sprawling wilderness of things has the effect of suddenly *assembling* everything within its purview. The wilderness "rose up to it" as it "took dominion everywhere," and suddenly it was no longer wild. Earth becomes world. The art work lets the earth and the world appear in their tension (Heraclitean "strife"): men, now suddenly *ek*-sisting in the tension thus opened up, become released toward things as they are assembled into world. At the same time nothing in itself is altered; everything remains what it is. Similarly, in art works of a more complex kind, the assemblage also is more complex: it is assemblage in what Heidegger calls the "foursome"—earth, world, (mortal) men, and gods. In such an assemblage the entire drama of Dasein is unconcealed. Here too we become true (in response to that which is unconcealed) as we learn to *dwell* with freedom toward the foursome—learning how "to spare the earth, receive the sky, expect the gods, and have a capacity for death." [29] Only where language is, is there world. But language is what it is by virtue of the *logos*, which, understood after the aesthetic modes of *a-letheia*, is the "articulated openness within which everything is assembled" into world;[30] but this, in its turn, is that place of dwelling articulated by and through what others have called root metaphors. When a root metaphor dies, a world is lost, and we are too if we cannot release ourselves from idolatrous fixations upon the *forms* of our knowing.

"I believe," Kenneth Burke has said, and most felicitously, "in the right of every man to worship God in his own metaphor." There may, of course, be no alternative, save in the fact that we seek, in our metaphysical passion, for a Metaphor of metaphors; but this also must appear within the assemblages of the foursome— at the *crux*, that is, of the strife between *a-letheia* and the drama of the existential situation.

IV. THE DISCLOSURE OF THE UNDISCLOSED

If we revert now to our opening suggestion it will be seen that the "hub of ultimacy" and our ways of understanding it are central to these studies and in line with both the hermeneutic quest in religious thinking and with Heidegger's plea for truth as *a-letheia*. What is surprising is the way in which the movement of the question *through* these essays at once remains the same and brings about its own reversal, as though this too might be an "anecdote" of finite understanding.

In the first two essays, those of Brown and Ott, aphorism and dialogue are proposed as models for poetic knowing. Marías and Barfield, however, do not wish to restrict poetic form to aphorism, and Barfield, in observing that poetry implies a "crossing the threshold between two dimensions of consciousness" implicitly regards the dialogic model, in its personalistic form, as too *rational*istic to be fully open to the mystery of Being-in-ourselves. Then Burke and Allemann, employing models of drama and antimetaphor respectively, come up with symbols without meaning—if meaning implies a world behind the world to which our metaphoric bridging could significantly be anchored. Yet the centrality of the poetic is affirmed, and each investigation buttresses the ones that come before and after. What are we to make of these seeming contradictions and agreements?

Perhaps one's editorial responsibility is discharged when one points to the problem. But perhaps also one must point to that to which the problem points. When Brown asserts the need for a Dionysian Christianity, the mythos of drama, with its chthonic descent, is appealed to quite as firmly as in Burke, where poetic language, when complete, will take us "into-and-out-of [the complete play with its exhilaration as the close]." This movement will enter also into the dialogic drama once it is seen that the *persona* of "I" and "Thou" are masks through which the "soul may leap to what it then suddenly recognizes beyond the mask. *Finis tragoedia: incipit comoedia*," [31] as Joseph Campbell has said.

This was, for Nicholas of Cusa, a movement through the opposites to a recognition of the faceless Face behind all faces—not to be beheld through the forming of concepts, but rather through rapture: "In all faces is seen the Face of faces, veiled, and in a riddle; howbeit unveiled it is not seen, until above all faces a man enter into a certain secret and mystic silence where there is no knowledge or concept of a face. . . ." [32]

Heidegger also knows this silence and observes its presence behind and within our language, much as Allemann notes its presence between our words. Drama also is not wholly lacking in this silence between our words, though one is tempted to feel so in the seemingly passive and receptive form in which we are enjoined to let Being be. But the metaphors of unconcealment, of assemblage in the foursome are not without dramatic implications. What Christian *theo-poiesis* does is to effect disclosure through the crucial nexus of event, thereby making the crux of knowing, both morally and aesthetically, radically decisive in time. The drama of the Cross is implicit in our language whenever we cease to dwell poetically in the world: that is, whenever "meaning" is not disclosed, whenever the clichés of everydayness or abstraction fixate words. Fixation crucifies. The Cross occurs whenever Primordial Being is unheard, elided, or refused. This would imply that Christianity, in its historical forms, has progressively destroyed its own meanings through fixation of its language, brought about by reason of its capitulation to a grammar not its own. Therefore its metaphors no longer function, and its central symbol elicits no response. Allemann's analysis of metaphor discloses this. Metaphor in its Aristotelian mode is suddenly artificial; there is no extrinsic Other to which a metaphor

may appeal; but the *form* of this appealing remains fixated in our
language where we repeat its modes inexorably. The antimetaphor
works against this, and, *mirabile dictu*, exacts surprise and un-
concealments from our finite particulars by letting things be what
they are. Whereat fresh wonders shine and mystery appears precisely where we thought no *logos* lay concealed. From "the infinite
qualitative distinction between time and eternity, God and man"
of thirty years ago, we have suddenly come upon reversal into
radical immanence.

This is a vision of reality that begins with Heraclitus, for
whom *logos* not only meant *a-letheia*, as Heidegger reminds us, but
for whom it also meant utterance—as though the whole of things
were essentially the speech of Being. It knows that "*phusis* loves
to hide." Its symbols are the fire, the bow, the lyre. Its *logos* is a
presence that "steers all things through all things." Like Pascal's
cosmos, its center is everywhere and its circumference is nowhere.
But also it is like Augustine's discovery of God: He was nearer
to Augustine than Augustine was to himself. "Thou wert with me,
but I was not with Thee." It is out of this discrepancy, where the
Presence is not recognized, that the aboriginal crime is born. This
is the cleavage that we then inflict on all the world.

Rilke's sonnet comes to mind:

> *A god can do it. But how, tell me, shall*
> *a man follow him through the narrow lyre?*
> *His mind is cleavage. At the crossing of two*
> *heartways stands no temple for Apollo.*[23]

"At the crossing of two heartways stands no temple . . ." But, as
Norman Brown remarked, it is precisely there, at the crossing of our
heartways, that all our temples stand. Quite so. But Rilke's point is
that there is no temple *for Apollo*. Apollo is the sun-god, and, as
the sun-god, Apollo symbolizes the excessive rationalization of life.
The overemphasis of the *ratio* deletes the temple. We must go down
now, as Rilke sees, *with Orpheus* to reconcile the opposites of
"above" and "below" in all their manifold expressions. Orpheus can
go down and Orpheus can return by the power of his song. But:

> *Song, as you teach it, is not desire,*
> *not suing for something yet in the end attained;*
> *song is existence. Easy for the god.*
> *But when do we exist? And when does he*
> *spend upon our being the earth and the stars?*[34]

Gesang ist Dasein! Not song, which is a pressing for returns; not the coercing of the givenness of things.

> *Real singing is a different breath.*
> *A breath for nothing. A wafting in the god. A wind.*[85]

Rilke seems to be saying that we must learn, with trust, to be one with, a breathing with the inhale and exhale of Being, in order that "the god" may breathe through us, and we, through the translation of its breath into song, may be (as I have ventured to remark elsewhere) the eyes of becoming and a tongue for Being's utterance.

NOTES

1. Jean Giraudoux, *Tiger at the Gates.* Trans. Christopher Fry (New York: Oxford Univ. Press, 1955), p. 32.

2. Wallace Stevens, "Notes Toward a Supreme Fiction," III, in *The Collected Poems of Wallace Stevens* (New York: Alfred A. Knopf, 1954), p. 382.

3. For a résumé of the Continental and American discussion of the hermeneutic question in theology today, the reader is referred to the excellent introductory chapters of James M. Robinson in Volumes I and II of the "New Frontiers in Theology" series: Vol. I, *The Later Heidegger and Theology,* pp. 48-56, and Vol. II, *The New Hermeneutic,* pp. 1-77. This second volume contains papers presented at the First Consultation on Hermeneutics convened at Drew University in 1962. (Both volumes are edited by James M. Robinson and John B. Cobb, Jr., and are published by Harper & Row, New York, 1963 and 1964 respectively.)

4. *Ibid.,* I, 6; cf. also the essay by Heinrich Ott, "What Is Systematic Theology?", pp. 77*ff.*

5. Ludwig Wittgenstein: *Philosophical Investigations,* trans. G. E. M. Anscombe (Oxford: Basil Blackwell, 1958), p. 48e (# 115).

6. In "Theology as Ontology and History," in *New Frontiers,* I, 139f.

7. *Vide* Heinrich Ott: *Denken und Sein. Der Weg Martin Heideggers und der Weg der Theologie* (Zürich: EVZ-Verlag, 1959).

8. *Op. cit.,* p. 78.

9. *Ibid.,* p. 156

10. *Ibid.,* p. 156.

11. *Vide New Frontiers,* II, on "The New Hermeneutic," which contains the papers presented at that Consultation.

12. *Einführung in die Metaphysic* (Tübingen: Niemeyer, 1953), p. 7.

13. *Wort und Glaube* (Tübingen: J. C. F. Mohr, 1960), p. 359; cited in *New Frontiers*, I, 74n.

14. "Zeitschrift für Theologie und Kirche," Beiheft 2, 1961, p. 124; cited in *New Frontiers*, I, 74n.

15. *New Frontiers*, I, 5.

16. "Remembrance of the Poet," in Martin Heidegger: *Existence and Being*, with an introduction by Werner Brock (London: Vision Press Ltd., 1949), pp. 285-86.

17. Norman O. Brown, *Love's Body* (New York: Random House, 1966), p. 266.

18. Delmore Schwartz, "The Kingdom of Poetry," in *Summer Knowledge* New York: Doubleday, 1959), p. 189. Schwartz, in his later poetry, shows the influence of Heidegger, Rilke, and Hölderlin.

19. "In Lieblicher Bläue . . . ," in *Hölderlin, His Poems*, trans., with a critical study, by Michael Hamburger (New York: Pantheon, 1952), p. 263.

20. "Hölderlin and the Essence of Poetry," *Existence and Being*, p. 307.

21. Martin Heidegger, *Being and Time*, trans. John Macquarrie and Edward Robinson (London: SCM Press, 1962), p. 194 (H. 152).

22. *Ibid.*, p. 195 (H. 153).

23. W. H. Auden, "The Labyrinth," in *The Collected Poetry of W. H. Auden* (New York: Random House, 1945), p. 10.

24. Heidegger, *Being and Time*, p. 195.

25. *Ibid.*, p. 63 (H. 39).

26. *Ibid.*, p. 190 (H. 149).

27. *Ibid.*, p. 58 (H. 34).

28. *The Collected Poems of Wallace Stevens*, p. 76.

29. Vincent Vycinas, *Earth and Gods, An Introduction to the Philosophy of Martin Heidegger* (The Hague: Martinus Nijhoff, 1961), p. 15.

30. *Ibid.*, p. 83.

31. Joseph Campbell: *The Masks of God*, Vol. I, *Primitive Mythology* (New York: Viking, 1959), p. 51; cited from Nicholas of Cusa, *De Visione*, trans. Emma Gurney Salter (London: J. M. Dent; New York, E. P. Dutton, 1928), pp. 25-27.

32. *Ibid.*

33. Rainer Maria Rilke, *Sonnets to Orpheus*, I, 3, trans. by M. D. Herter Norton (New York: W. W. Norton, 1942), p. 21.

34. *Ibid.*

35. *Ibid.*

I

**RELIGION AND
THE SOURCE
OF MEANING**

Ἀγχιβασίη. . . .
So könnte denn das Staunen das Verschlossene öffnen?
Nach der Art des Wartens . . .
wenn dies ein gelassenes ist.

—MARTIN HEIDEGGER

❊ THE PROBLEM, as stated in the introduction, is whether or not a nonobjectifying language is possible. In the study of religion this problem may be taken as one of discovering a mode of human language appropriate for spiritual truth. This implies that some modes of human discourse constrict the meaning of religion into narrow, finite perspectives.

Both authors writing in this section agree that literalistic modes of interpretation and all forms of positivism are inappropriate to spiritual truth. Norman O. Brown and Heinrich Ott reject the inadequate hermeneutics typified, according to Martin Heidegger, in the entire tradition of philosophy from Plato to Nietzsche. In the epigraph above, Heidegger calls for a "going on the way toward meaning" (ἀγχιβασίη), which would be an opening of meaning by way of wonder, if the wonder is a waiting with acceptance. The question remains: What mode of language will manifest the openness for acceptance, the continually reformational quality of "being on the way," and the glory of wonder?

In *Life Against Death* (1959) Norman O. Brown called for a psychologically informed version of what Jacob Boehme termed *die sensualische Sprache*, "sensual speech." Such language, the language of poets, embodies the spiritual, speaks the unspeakable, incarnates meaning, introduces the unconscious into consciousness. In a recent work, *Love's Body* (1966), Brown is more specific about the form *die sensualische Sprache* may take. He says, in a phrase that exhibits its content in its own form: "Words taken out of time into eternity: aphorism the form of eternity."

Brown has indicated that the essay "Apocalypse" is the "missing item" in "a voyage begun with *Life Against Death*" and continued in *Love's Body*. This essay shows its author's own "being on the way" to an answer for the problem of non-objectifying discourse. It shows not only the movement that identifies aphorism as the form of *die sensualische Sprache*, not only the affirmation of wonder in waiting, but also, as Brown himself says, the attempt "to find again the mysteries" now lost in a time when religion, understood as mysticism, has "degenerated into mechanism." Like Heidegger, Brown feels that "order as we have known it is crippling." Through the power of the imagination, "civilization has to be renewed by the discovery of new mysteries."

Heinrich Ott, though he agrees with Brown and Heidegger in dismissing all positivism as objectifying, as a constricting mode of language for spiritual truth, takes a path different from Brown in his quest for conveying a nonobjectifying discourse. In an essay he contributed to *The Later Heidegger and Theology* in 1961, Ott calls for a language of wonder to replace past theologies of logical dialectics. And in the essay presented here, he proposes *the dialogue* as the model for such an authentically "religious language."

In explaining the significance of dialogic discourse, he rejects the organismic model for language taken from natural, evolutionary ways of thinking. In this expression of preference Ott demonstrates the difference between himself and Brown, who in *Love's Body* appeals to evolution and its radical form, revolution, as the full meaning of the work of aphorism and poetic imagination. Ott indicates that his own preference for dialogic language (as opposed to Brown's aphoristic language) is motivated by the way in which dialogue preserves the inter-

4

personal and historical dimensions of religious faith, thereby remaining open to "the mysterious many-layered, always questionable total complex of man's historical experience."

Therefore, the two following chapters are different approaches to the rediscovery of a mode of language that fully embodies the meaning of spiritual truth. One way leads toward a mystical understanding of religion; the other, toward a historical and personal understanding of religion. Both ways, however, lead away from the logical and literal and move toward wonder.

1

Norman O. Brown:
Apocalypse: The
Place of Mystery
in the Life
of the Mind [1]

I DIDN'T KNOW whether I should appear before you—there is a time to show and a time to hide; there is a time to speak, and also a time to be silent. What time is it? It is fifteen years since H. G. Wells said Mind is at the End of its Tether—with a frightful queerness come into life: there is no way out or around or through, he said; it is the end. It is because I think mind is at the end of its tether that I would be silent. It is because I think there is a way out—a way down and out—the title of Mr. John Senior's new book on the occult tradition in literature[2]—that I will speak.

Mind at the end of its tether: I can guess what some of you are thinking—*his* mind is at the end of its tether—and this could be; it scares me but it deters me not. The alternative to mind is certainly madness. Our greatest blessings, says Socrates in the *Phaedrus*, come to us by way of madness—provided, he adds, that the madness comes from the god. Our real choice is between holy and unholy madness: open your eyes and look around you—madness is in the saddle anyhow, Freud is the measure of our unholy madness, as Nietzsche is the prophet of the holy madness, of Dionysus, the mad truth. Dionysus has returned to his native Thebes; mind—at the end of its tether—

is another Pentheus, up a tree. Resisting madness can be the maddest way of being mad.

And there is a way out—the blessed madness of the maenad and the bacchant: "Blessed is he who has the good fortune to know the mysteries of the gods, who sanctifies his life and initiates his soul, a bacchant on the mountains, in holy purifications." It is possible to be mad and to be unblest; but it is not possible to get the blessing without the madness; it is not possible to get the illuminations without the derangement. Derangement is disorder: the Dionysian faith is that order as we have known it is crippling, and for cripples; that what is past is prologue; that we can throw away our crutches and discover the supernatural power of walking; that human history goes from man to superman.

No superman I; I come to you not as one who has supernatural powers, but as one who seeks for them, and who has some notions which way to go to find them.

Sometimes—most times—I think that the way down and out leads out of the university, out of the academy. But perhaps it is rather that we should recover the academy of earlier days— the Academy of Plato in Athens, the Academy of Ficino in Florence, Ficino who says,

> The spirit of the god Dionysus was believed by the ancient theologians and Platonists to be the ecstasy and abandon of disencumbered minds, when partly by innate love, partly at the instigation of the god, they transgress the natural limits of intelligence and are miraculously transformed into the beloved god himself: where, inebriated by a certain new draft of nectar and by an immeasurable joy, they rage, as it were, in bacchic frenzy. In the drunkenness of this Dionysian wine, our Dionysius (the Areopagite) expresses his exultation. He pours forth enigmas, he sings in dithyrambs. To penetrate the profundity of his meanings, to imitate his quasi-Orphic manner of speech, we too require the divine fury.

At any rate the point is first of all to find again the mysteries. By which I do not mean simply the sense of wonder— that sense of wonder which is indeed the source of all true philosophy—by mystery I mean secret and occult; therefore unpublishable; therefore outside the university as we know it; but not outside Plato's Academy, or Ficino's.

Why are mysteries unpublishable? First because they cannot be put into words, at least not the kinds of words which earned you your Phi Beta Kappa keys. Mysteries display themselves in words only if they can remain concealed; this is poetry, isn't it? We must return to the old doctrine of the Platonists and Neo-Platonists, that poetry is veiled truth; as Dionysus is the god who is both manifest and hidden; and as John Donne declared, with the Pillar of Fire goes the Pillar of Cloud. This is also the new doctrine of Ezra Pound, who says: "Prose is not education but the outer courts of the same. Beyond its doors are the mysteries. Eleusis. Things not to be spoken save in secret. The mysteries self-defended, the mysteries that cannot be revealed. Fools can only profane them. The dull can neither penetrate the secretum nor divulge it to others." [3] The mystic academies, whether Plato's or Ficino's, knew the limitations of words and drove us on beyond them, to go over, to go under, to the learned ignorance, in which God is better honored and loved by silence than by words, and better seen by closing the eyes to images than by opening them.

And second, mysteries are unpublishable because only some can see them, not all. Mysteries are intrinsically esoteric, and as such an offense to democracy: is not publicity a democratic principle? Publication makes it republican—a thing of the people. The pristine academies were esoteric and aristocratic, self-consciously separate from the profane vulgar. Democratic resentment denies that there can be anything that can't be seen by everybody; in the democratic academy truth is subject to public verification; truth is what any fool can see. This is what is meant by the so-called scientific method: so-called science is that attempt to democratize knowledge—the attempt to substitute method for insight, mediocrity for genius, by getting a standard operating procedure. The great equalizers dispensed by the scientific method are the tools, those analytical tools. The miracle of genius is replaced by the standardized mechanism. But fools with tools are still fools, and don't let your Phi Beta Kappa key fool you. Tibetan prayer wheels are another way of arriving at the same result: the degeneration of mysticism into mechanism—so that any fool can do it. Perhaps the advantage is with Tibet: for there the mechanism is external while the mind is left vacant; and vacancy is not the worst condition of the mind. And the resultant prayers make no futile claim to originality or immortality; being nonexistent, they do not have to be catalogued or stored.

The sociologist Simmel sees showing and hiding, secrecy and publicity, as two poles, like Yin and Yang, between which societies oscillate in their historical development. I sometimes think I see that civilizations originate in the disclosure of some mystery, some secret; and expand with the progressive publication of their secret; and end in exhaustion when there is no longer any secret, when the mystery has been divulged, that is to say profaned. The whole story is illustrated in the difference between ideogram and alphabet. The alphabet is indeed a democratic triumph; and the enigmatic ideogram, as Ezra Pound has taught us, is a piece of mystery, a piece of poetry, not yet profaned. And so there comes a time—I believe we are in such a time—when civilization has to be renewed by the discovery of new mysteries, by the undemocratic but sovereign power of the imagination, by the undemocratic power which makes poets the unacknowledged legislators of mankind, the power which makes all things new.

The power which makes all things new is magic. What our time needs is mystery: what our time needs is magic. Who would not say that only a miracle can save us? In Tibet the degree-granting institution is, or used to be, the College of Magic Ritual. It offers courses in such fields as clairvoyance and telepathy; also (attention physics majors) internal heat: internal heat is a yoga bestowing supernatural control over body temperature. Let me succumb for a moment to the fascination of the mysterious East and tell you of the examination procedure for the course in internal heat. Candidates assemble naked, in midwinter, at night, on a frozen Himalayan lake. Beside each one is placed a pile of wet frozen undershirts; the assignment is to wear, until they are dry, as many as possible of these undershirts before dawn. Where the power is real, the test is real, and the grading system dumfoundingly objective. I say no more. I say no more; Eastern Yoga does indeed demonstrate the existence of supernatural powers, but it does not have the particular power our Western society needs: or rather I think that each society has access only to its own proper powers; or rather each society will only get the kind of power it knows how to ask for.

The Western consciousness has always asked for freedom; the human mind was born free, or at any rate born to be free, but everywhere it is in chains; and now at the end of its tether. It will take a miracle to free the human mind: because the chains are magical in the first place. We are in bondage to authority outside ourselves: most obviously in bondage to the authority of books. There is a Transcendentalist anticipation of what I want to say in Emerson's Phi Beta Kappa address on the American Scholar:

> The books of an older period will not fit this. Yet hence arises a grave mischief. The sacredness which attaches to the act of creation, the act of thought, is transferred to the record. . . . Instantly the book becomes noxious: the guide is a tyrant. The sluggish and perverted mind of the multitude . . . having once received this book, stands upon it, and makes an outcry if it is destroyed. Colleges are built on it. . . . Meek young men grow up in libraries. . . . Hence, instead of Man Thinking, we have the bookworm. . . . I had better never see a book than to be warped by its attraction clean out of my own orbit, and make a satellite instead of a system. The one thing in the world, of value, is the active soul.[4]

How far the university is from that ideal is the measure of the defeat of our American dream.

This bondage to books compels us not to see with our own eyes; compels us to see with the eyes of the dead, with dead eyes. Whitman, likewise in a Transcendentalist sermon, says, "You shall no longer take things at second or third hand, nor look through the eyes of the dead, nor feed on the specters in books." There is a hex on us, the specters in books, the authority of the past; and to exorcise these ghosts is the great work of magical self-liberation. Then the eyes of the spirit would be-

come one with the eyes of the body, and god would be in us, not
outside. God in us: *entheos:* enthusiasm; this is the essence of
the holy madness. In the fire of the holy madness even books
lose their gravity, and let themselves go up into the flame:
"Properly," says Ezra Pound, "we should read for power. Man
reading should be man intensely alive. The book should be a ball
of light in one's hand." [5]

I began with the name of Dionysus; let me be permitted to
end with the name of Christ: for the power I seek is also Christian. Nietzsche indeed said the whole question was Dionysus
versus Christ; but only the fool will take these as mutually exclusive opposites. There is a Dionysian Christianity, an apoc-
alyptic Christianity, a Christianity of miracles and revelations.
And there always have been some Christians for whom the age
of miracle and revelation is not over; Christians who claim the
spirit; enthusiasts. The power I look for is the power of enthusiasm; as condemned by John Locke; as possessed by George
Fox, the Quaker; through whom the houses were shaken; who
saw the channel of blood running down the streets of the city
of Litchfield; to whom, as a matter of fact, was even given the
magic internal heat—"The fire of the Lord was so in my feet,
and all around me, that I did not matter to put on my shoes any
more."

Read again the controversies of the seventeenth century and
discover our choice: we are either in an age of miracles, says
Hobbes, miracles which authenticate fresh revelations; or else
we are in an age of reasoning from already received Scripture.
Either miracle or Scripture. George Fox, who came up in spirit
through the flaming sword into the paradise of God, so that all
things were new, he being renewed to the state of Adam which
he was in before he fell, sees that none can read John's words
aright, and with a true understanding of them, but in and with
the same divine spirit by which John spake them, and by his
burning shining light which is sent from God. Thus the authority of the past is swallowed up in new creation; the word
is made flesh. We see with our own eyes and to see with our
own eyes is second sight. To see with our own eyes is second
sight.

Twofold always. May God us keep
From single vision and Newton's sleep.[6]

NOTES

1. The following was delivered as the Phi Beta Kappa Oration at Columbia University on May 31, 1960, and was printed in *Harper's Magazine*, CCXXII (May, 1961), 46-49.

2. John Senior, *The Way Down and Out: The Occult in Symbolist Literature* (Ithaca: Cornell University Press, 1959).

3. Ezra Pound, *Guide to Kulchur* (New York: New Directions, n.d.), pp. 144-45.

4. Ralph Waldo Emerson, *Nature, Addresses, and Lectures* (Boston: Houghton, Mifflin and Co., 1894), pp. 90-91.

5. Ezra Pound, *op. cit.*, p. 55.

6. William Blake, *Letters*, ed. Geoffrey Keynes (New York: Macmillan, 1956), p. 79.

2

Heinrich Ott:
Hermeneutics and
Personhood

IN HIS BOOK *Unterwegs zur Sprache* (1959) Martin Heidegger
defined the proper and central theme of his thinking as "the
hermeneutical" (*das Hermeneutische*), as, for instance, on page
97f:

> Hermeneutik meint in *S. u. Z.* weder die Lehre von der Ausle-
> gungskunst noch das Auslegen selbst, vielmehr den Versuch, das
> Wesen der Auslegung allererst aus dem Hermeneutischen zu
> bestimmen.[1]

The context of this utterance is a dialogue with a Japanese
scholar (in the essay, "*Aus einem Gespräch von der Sprache*").
The question of being is not at issue in the essay, since being
would not be an appropriate theme in a dialogue with East
Asian thought. Instead, the "hermeneutical" appears as an even
more original theme for Heidegger than the question of being.

In this paper, I would like to try as a theologian to pursue
this comprehensive theme, "the hermeneutical," a few steps
further. The basic model of the hermeneutical, as we can see
in the Heideggerian context, and as Hans-Georg Gadamer in
his important book, *Wahrheit und Methode*, pointed out very
clearly, as opposed to every form of historical positivism is the

dialogue. Every hermeneutical event is a dialogue and hence presupposes at least two concerned dialogue partners.

In saying that, we have gained a perspective which allows us to see together both large question-complexes which must occupy us in theology today above all: the problem of hermeneutics and the problem of personality (namely, the personhood of God and the personhood of man in the ordinary and in the extraordinary reality of his existence). Indeed, both spheres of questioning have a common root. Or, more precisely: they are rooted in each other, indissolubly connected, so that they interpret each other.

Therefore, our thesis is quite simple: The model and basic structure of every hermeneutical event is the dialogue. (In saying that, we have to conceive the notion of "hermeneutical event" as broadly as possible: so broadly, that it covers the major part—perhaps, even, in the last analysis, the whole—of the reality which surrounds us and which concerns us in any way.) The dialogue is a personal, that is to say, an interpersonal, event. Therefore we have to understand and to interpret the essence of the hermeneutical out of the primary experience of personhood, namely the primary experience of personal being-together. On the other hand, personhood also must be understood and interpreted out of the hermeneutical: in personal being-together it is not only a question of a simple being-side-by-side or so-called "overagainstness" of two or more chiefly isolated, free and so-called "personal" subjects, who have the freedom to begin and mold relations with each other. Thought of in that way, the reality of personhood would plainly not yet be understood. Rather, persons are together in that they stand together under the claim of a common "subject matter" (whatever this may be—something everyday-like or something extraordinary), in which and confronting which they are then first able to understand each other.

So much for my thesis. It is not my intention, in the following consideration, to prove this thesis in the proper sense. I think, nevertheless, that there is a good bit of evidence for it. Rather, by means of several observations out of different thematic areas, I would like to try to make this thesis more concrete. In a first main part I would like to make some remarks concerning the old theological notion of *implicit faith*, of *fides implicita*, with reference to which we can exemplify very well the close connection of the hermeneutical and personhood, assuming that we first understand this notion more profoundly than the customary Catholic and Protestant classroom theology used to do. In a second main part, on the basis of everyday experiences of dialogue, several remarks appropriate to a *phenomenology of dialogue* as the personal basic model of all hermeneutics should be made. Also, these remarks have a theological connotation that will appear occasionally: they have originated through the endeavor to find the appropriate method for the interpretation of the work of Dietrich Bonhoeffer, who, although he died twenty years ago, is nonetheless today in the deepest sense more our theological contemporary than many others who still are alive. So then he too must be interpreted as a contemporary with whom we carry on a living dialogue today. Also, the work of Dietrich Bonhoeffer poses for us a specific problem of hermeneutical methodology because of its very fragmentary character, mainly in its last period.

REMARKS CONCERNING THE NOTION OF IMPLICIT FAITH

The notion *fides implicita*, as we know, marks an old controversy between the Catholic and Protestant understanding of faith. As opposed to the Roman conception of an implicit faith of the individual in that which the Church believes, Protestant theology posed the necessity of being conscious of the faith that we confess. However, Calvin (*Institutes* III, II, 4) admits that in a certain sense—that is to say so long as we are pilgrims in this aeon of darkness and error—our faith is indeed an implicit one. Faith as faith within historicity, within historical finitude, is essentially implicit!

The structure of faith as *fides implicita* can in two aspects be understood more profoundly and be explained more precisely: one aspect is hermeneutics and the other that of personhood. Let us consider both of them.

The Hermeneutical Aspect

The hermeneutical aspect of implicit faith is to be understood from the fact that faith is essentially a knowledge. And to be sure, it is a kind of knowledge that is more to be compared with the knowledge of the historical sciences than with the knowledge of the natural sciences. The characteristic feature of knowledge within the historical sciences is that it is an *understanding* of an always specific *content of meaning,* an understanding not primarily growing out of a distanced observation (although distanced and unprejudiced observation has its important place here, too) but rather out of a historical encounter between the subject matter and the one wanting to know. This kind of knowledge I would like to call hermeneutical knowledge. We encounter, in a certain sense, the structure of *fides implicita* as an implicit knowledge revealing itself step by step in all hermeneutical knowledge.

This, then, is the way I always perceive a historical phenomenon: I understand it first in a preliminary way, and then the more experience I have with it and the more I also reflect about those experiences, the more clearly and profoundly I understand. Through each living experience my total image of the phenomenon is affected again and again and consequently more or less modified. The image changes without thereby losing its identity (always assuming that I didn't begin with a fundamental misunderstanding that, at some moment, must be fundamentally corrected by a particular experience).

My knowledge of the subject matter in the realm of hermeneutical knowledge does not so much grow in volume in the process of knowing, but rather in *depth.* In this sense we may say: *In my first knowledge of the subject matter I already knew implicitly all that which I later learned in addition.* This last statement, which may sound very bold, must be understood with all necessary reservations. It can certainly be pressed so far that it loses every reasonable meaning. But if it be correctly understood, it will show something of the specific nature of hermeneutical knowledge.

I would like to explain the meaning of this sentence by an

example: I read a literary work and by reading gain a first total image. Afterwards I have new experiences with the same subject matter, and so I learn many things in addition. I read, for instance, interpretations of the work, I learn something about its origin, about the author, and about the other works of the writer, and his whole intellectual world; perhaps I even meet the author personally, etc. All this is new for me and modifies my image of the work. So the latter continually changes, yet nonetheless remains identical with itself. Maybe I could already infer or faintly sense many things from the work itself, while many things I could not. And nevertheless, my knowledge of all of it, even of that which is totally new, will be characterized as re-cognition: "Aha!"—I shall say to myself in learning a new detail—"Now I understand better what I then already understood, could have been able to sense faintly, or even: that implicitly I already understood in that I read the work and it made an impression upon me and I gained an image of it, an image which is confirmed for me even when it is modified and changed by new impressions." The encounter with the work thus in a certain sense continues. The implicit knowledge given from the outset makes itself explicit step by step, however not simply of itself, but under the influence of new encounters with the same subject matter. Because the encounter goes on, I recognize constantly in everything new the spirit that had already touched me at the beginning.

The "subject matter" of faith, God in His revelation, is therefore a historical event (historical in the sense of *Geschichtlichkeit*). Faith is, as we know, not blind, not a blind risk, but it is a knowledge: a historical (therefore hermeneutical) knowledge of this unique and eschatological event. Theology is the understanding and reflecting articulation of this knowledge of faith. Therefore it appears understandable that faith, in existential experience, as well as in the theological articulation of its knowledge, is always implicit faith, corresponding to the structure of all hermeneutical knowledge.

To be sure, we do not deduce this statement from a general definition of hermeneutical knowledge. Rather, theology, on the basis of its own competence and in view of its own subject matter, has to decide about its self-understanding. And I think it has already decided about that long ago, even before such considerations were made about the nature of hermeneutical knowledge in general. Of course, it may rather be that the genuinely theological notion of *fides implicita* can appropriately make us aware of the general structure of the hermeneutical. Now, however, since we have discovered a certain parallelism or common structure of faith knowledge and hermeneutical knowledge, this insight may become helpful for further clearing up the state of affairs in faith and theology.

Two remarks for the sake of precision may close this section: (1) The notion and state of affairs of *fides implicita* has occasionally been described by *an analogy to an organism:* As a bud already contains what afterwards reveals itself as a flower, as vegetative life already carries its entelechy in itself, so it is also in implicit faith with respect to explicit faith. The same analogy—according to our considerations earlier—may be applied to all hermeneutical knowledge. As seductive, however, as it may seem at first glance, this analogy nonetheless is not in every respect adequate to the subject matter, since the implicit knowledge of faith is developed not on its own strength, but through new encounters, not by an inner drive, but by impulses from outside. The process of explication here is not an organic one, but an historical one. Here, there is no entelechy in the strict sense; the horizon of the future remains open. Nevertheless there is here a continuity and a gradual explication toward an always greater clarity. The character of historicity and the open horizon of the future does not, by any means, signify a splitting of history into isolated events. In this restricted sense the analogy of organism and of organic growth may be legitimate.

(2) A better model for explaining *fides implicita* than the organic one is that of *dialogue*. Dialogue, as we already pointed out, is a hermeneutical phenomenon, probably *the* hermeneutical phenomenon, and we can reflect about its essence on the basis of our experiences in the area of hermeneutical knowledge. The relationship between God and man, between revelation and faith, is one of dialogue. Certainly, this is a

dialogue of a unique kind to be distinguished from every other, but in spite of these significant differences, it seems to be justified here to speak of a dialogue. God speaks (through the word of His revelation, documented in the Holy Scriptures, mediated by the proclamation of the church; of course God also speaks through the historical events themselves, but here we can only perceive him properly if we interpret the historical events out of the Word). Man responds (in prayer, in his praying existence, in actions and thoughts, which grow out of his faith). Secondarily then, the reverse happens: man speaks and God answers. There eventuates a real dialogue and consequently a real history, a real history and consequently a real dialogue. Obviously important questions remain yet unanswered: how this unique dialogue with the invisible God, the Creator and Saviour of the world, occurs *in concreto*, in view of its difference from all other dialogues. At this point, however, we can say this much: to the essence of a dialogue belongs the gradual explication of the implicit. Thus, I stand from the outset of a dialogue already under the claim of my dialogue partner. In the process of the dialogue (assuming that we stay close to our subject matter) this claim becomes clearer step by step. It displays itself with ever increasing clarity—this, however, not in the way of an organic development, but in that this claim in the course of the dialogue meets me again and again from outside, from him "over-against" me, anew and yet as the same claim, and in this way the encounter of the dialogue is lived and carried through.

The Personal Aspect

The personal aspect of the implicit faith results from the fact that God and man stand over against each other as persons. Where man does not yet know consciously about God, this personal relationship is, so to speak, one-sided; where, however, man enters into the luminous sphere of revelation, the relationship becomes mutually conscious and a proper situation of conscious dialogue arises.

It will here be helpful if we juxtapose the observations we are able to make about human interpersonal relations with our attempt to clarify the relationship with God. So we can say, for instance: a real, deep human encounter and relationship consists in that "there is much to be said to one another." There is much to be said to one another, even when the relationship takes place mostly in silence or without many words. All that which is to be said or will have to be said is, as it were, implicit in the relationship itself. The persons involved need only to look at one another, or to walk beside one another or to work together, and they know, silently, that they mean something to each other, for instance that they can rely upon one another, or that each has something important to expect from the other—and so precisely that there is much to be said to one another—even if one is unable for the moment to articulate it. The personal relationship between men is from the outset located in the sphere of language. Language and personhood belong together. And so one will articulate at a given time that which one has to say to another and this will, whenever it is an essential word, arise out of the relationship and will explicate and at the same time modify that relationship. In the process, corresponding to the situation in which it is spoken and to the subject matter to which it refers, it will certainly always be a new word. Nevertheless, it will be spoken out of the same human relationship and, reflecting back upon it, will determine its history. Thus, the personal relationship is a source of language, and language is the realm in which the history of the relationship comes to pass.

In the same way faith, as personal relationship with God, is a source of language, and the language of faith is the realm for the history of faith. From this nature of faith as a relationship between I and Thou it follows that faith is necessarily always *fides implicita*. In a personal relationship there is always more contained than what is articulated in words and thoughts. What is expressed in words never exhausts what is contained within the relationship. And yet the relationship lives out of the event of language. It must make itself explicit within the realm of language, but this not once and for all from a conclusive standpoint, but so that precisely through this explication history occurs.

So faith in the course of its history makes explicit that which is in it implicitly as in a personal relationship with God. Whatever faith makes explicit in the course of this history of explication (in which theology as the thinking of faith, as reflecting articulation, plays a decisive role) is not faith's own property, which would be immanent in a mere human attitude confronting God, but what becomes explicit this way is the reality of the *relationship itself*. It is that which, *between* I and Thou, *between* God and man, is posed by God himself as the reality of the relationship. This "between" is the reality of the revelation itself—for the notion "revelation" means nothing other than the personal relationship between God and men, posed and made possible by God, "one-sidedly."

REMARKS CONCERNING THE PHENOMENOLOGY OF DIALOGUE

We lack up to now a comprehensive phenomenology of dialogue. And yet this would be of the greatest importance for every kind of hermeneutical consideration and especially for the practice of hermeneutics in the actual process of interpretation, whether in Biblical exegesis or in understanding that spoken by philosophers or poets.

Here we can make only a few observations without any claim to completeness or systematic order. We shall begin each of six points from a quite simple state-of-affairs that each of us has already verified within our everyday experience of disciplined discussion, and then each time we will ask what that state of affairs might signify for the method of interpretation (hence, for "hermeneutics" in the traditional and narrow sense). In each case Bonhoeffer and his work, which on the one hand is so significant today and on the other so fragmentary, may serve us as a paradigm.

Let me say from the outset that I consider that which will be shown to us only as structures of dialogue occurring in certain cases, the knowledge of which may be hermeneutically helpful in such cases, but not as general rules which would be valid always and everywhere. The life of dialogue is too complex to allow for such things as general rules.

1. We understand our dialogue partner when we succeed in formulating that which he has to say in words that are not his own words.

Understanding demands a paraphrase. This can be explicit, so that I actually succeed in paraphrasing, or it can be implicit, so that I know each time that I would be able to. If I am not able at all to paraphrase the thought process that meets me, there is at least no warrant that I have understood. Perhaps I am then only repeating the words within which the thought process found its first articulation, while its meaning, the way it aims at the subject matter, remains foreign to me. Thus, a too-obedient disciple who only repeats words and moves with a certain ability and a great obedience within the realm of a classroom terminology is not yet really understanding. For the teacher whose terminology in such a case is only imitated, the student has not become a real partner in the dialogue who, for his part, might aid the teacher toward knowledge of the subject matter. In this sense, the possibility for continued dialogue is a symptom of real understanding.

The weakness of presentations and interpretations of a text often consists in the fact that they keep too closely to the terminology and diction of the text to be interpreted—or, in other words, that they don't paraphrase.

An appropriate paraphrase presupposes that I bring into the game my own past: the presuppositions that are familiar to me, the notional tools to which I am accustomed, or that seem to me to be useful, in order to express with their help the thought process of the other, to appropriate it, to fit it into the context of my own search for truth, or in other words, to let it speak to me. If, then, the dialogue partner recognizes in my paraphrase his own thought, then we have understood each other and have become companions on the same path, at least to a certain extent. But, then, everything does not remain the same for me either. It is not that I simply "consume" his thought, fitting it smoothly into the arsenal of my former notions. In this case I simply would not yet have understood. Rather, my notions change and are forced open, my presuppositions are modified and my horizon widened; I gain new dimensions of understanding and expression. It is precisely by putting at stake what I bring with me into the encounter that I myself am changed and am lifted above what I bring as my own. Thus. I come a step closer to the truth that I seek and that seeks me.

Paraphrase is an unavoidable task in the conversation with one's contemporaries, with present dialogue partners. Each of us unavoidably brings with him into dialogue his personal horizon of thinking, conditioned by origin and future, by personal intellectual experience. Also, in actual conversation each of us always places the emphasis in a somewhat different place and likes to use his own concepts. This must not mean a contradiction insofar as the subject matter is concerned, but rather a vivid competition in our wrestling for clarity. Because of this everyone who participates in the conversation will, by means of his own tools, experiences, and horizons, be able to contribute something to the clarification of the subject matter that concerns the other partner as well. And it is certainly a mistake to believe that one and the same subject matter can only be expressed in one and the same way.

Dietrich Bonhoeffer, for instance, doesn't speak of existentialist interpretation, and occasionally he expressly separates himself from Bultmann's demythologizing. This does not, however, exclude the possibility that the methodological notion of an existentialist interpretation (which can be defined in different ways) can be an appropriate tool to describe that which really was Bonhoeffer's motif, namely the nonreligious interpretation of Biblical notions, and perhaps to clarify it further beyond what Bonhoeffer expressly said. Nor does Bonhoeffer speak anywhere of a "supernatural existential," but this doesn't make impossible using this notion of modern Catholic theology (Karl Rahner) meaningfully for the purpose of further thinking through the Bonhoefferian beginnings in the understanding of human reality and of Christology. Of course, only in the pursuing of the dialogue will it appear which of the notions, experiences, and dimensions are appropriate to the subject matter encompassed by Bonhoeffer and are suited to it. Thus, we must subject the notions to a critical examination within the dialogue. In that way, then, the model of present dialogue, of actual conversation becomes helpful in order to clear up the exegetical situation with respect to a certain text.

2. If we contradict our dialogue partner or attribute a different weight to his utterances, this is not necessarily an expression of disagreement, but rather can be the expression of a common searching for a truth binding us both.

In a vivid conversation it should be possible to say to our partner: "I think I sense what you want to say. But in your place I would not use the notion that you just mentioned, because I believe that it rather obscures the subject matter; I would not go too far in the direction you mentioned a little while ago; of your two last arguments I only consider one helpful, but I think I could suggest another . . ." etc. That such a discourse is possible and meaningful, adequate and not arbitrary, is based upon the fact that the notions and thoughts we accomplish in our essentially dialogical thinking have their center of gravity, their meaning, their aim, essentially not in themselves, in the formulation as such, in the "letter," but outside of themselves, in that which is to be thought and that which is to be spoken, in the subject matter toward which they aim. Notions and thoughts therefore are not essentially closed, isolated intellectual forms, but are open toward their subject matter, and pointing to it.

In a similar fashion, then, the notions and thought processes of Dietrich Bonhoeffer are not closed, to be recorded and appreciated as static patterns, as unchangeably being thus and so as fixed positions, which we could either affirm or reject or partly affirm and partly reject, but they have, like all essential notions and thought processes, their proper dynamic. They are functions of a movement of seeking and therefore open toward their subject matter, which, in the case of Bonhoeffer, is in our opinion still the subject matter and problem of present theology, in fact without significant change of perspective. Accordingly, it seems to be appropriate that we, moved by Bonhoeffer, begin to search together with him and in the process remain free to make our own proposals toward solutions. If, for instance, we contradict Bonhoeffer in part, if we do not consider especially fruitful his attempt to establish a particular philosophy of history or his doctrine about the four mandates, and do not build them into our own way of thinking, we do not necessarily speak against Bonhoeffer, but for him and with him. For Bonhoeffer is for us not a representative of his own particular "position" or "theory," which he himself invented (if we would understand him this way he would be dead and no longer a real dialogue partner); rather, he is for us a thinker on the way towards truth.

3. We will verify our understanding of the word and the intention of our dialogue partner with respect to the subject matter itself and not only with respect to the affirmation. We understand our dialogue partner, then, if we understand better the subject matter with which both he and we are concerned.

An utterance in a dialogue is not a final position, but rather a *stade*. The utterance itself is essentially shaped in this way. It would be a misunderstanding to consider it as a final and closed theory. The utterance asks for an answer, which must also be a critical one. It is essentially a challenge and a call that demands an answer. And this, to be sure, is also the case (seen from the viewpoint of the dialogical essence of all thinking) even if the utterance itself seems to understand itself as final and intransigent. An utterance needs a critical, examining response in order to reach—to speak scholastically—its own essential perfection.

Therefore I can't understand a person if I only understand his isolated "opinion" as such, without understanding in the process what he *means* by his opinion. If, however, I have become aware of the subject matter that concerns him (and this not only in a rough, general way, but aware of it in the specific manner in which it concerns him) only then have I really understood him; only then has his utterance really reached me.

In a dialogical interpretation of Bonhoeffer, then, which takes him not as a witness of the past but as a witness for the present, two critical issues will probably have to be discussed at once; an interpretation of Bonhoeffer will be forced to face two different demands of verification. On the one hand, the listener will ask that the correctness, the adequacy, of the grasping of

Bonhoeffer's thought be verified. On the other hand, however, an interpreter who proceeds in a dialogical way will be challenged to show the truth of his own utterance with reference to the subject matter, of his own contribution in his conversation with Bonhoeffer, whom he endeavors to interpret. Both demands are quite understandable. The interpreter must be able to respond to both. If we, for instance, speak of Bonhoeffer's Christological universalism and seek to evaluate this as the profoundest interpretation of the Christ-event as well as of reality in general, this is on the one hand an exegetical thesis, on the other hand, however, a systematic thesis of our own to which we came by following Bonhoeffer.

I believe, however, that we can deduce from the general experience of conversation that both demands of verification and both processes of verification can indeed be distinguished, but in the practice of dialogue they almost always form one single process of work or thought. It is certainly conceivable that I say to my partner in dialogue: "You are absolutely right when you say that, . . ." but that he answers, "You misunderstood me . . . That's not at all what I meant." Then in principle I can still be right in what I considered as the opinion of the other and which I appropriated myself. But my interpretation of the other was not correct. So the question of interpretation and the question of the subject matter itself are separated. But normally it will be the other way around. The dialogue partner (if I really followed him) will tell me: "You about hit upon what I wanted to say myself; in a way you even said it more precisely, and so we have come a step closer to the truth." Then, perhaps, he himself will again make my formulation more precise. And so the dialogue goes on.

It may even be (and this probably occurs quite often) that only after a certain length of time one of the dialogue partners becomes aware that the other one has thought further the meaning of his own intention. It may also be that a third person comes to this insight first. When someone has once made a meaningful statement, he, in a certain sense, loses control of it. It is no longer a matter of his exclusive intellectual private property, at his personal disposal; rather what is expressed is and remains as a tendency of meaning delivered over to public discussion, and everybody else is free to draw appropriate conclusions. (In this sense the well-known statement is true: one can understand somebody else better than he understands himself.) So it must, in the last analysis, be decided with respect to the subject matter itself, whether I understood and interpreted somebody correctly or not. The discussion of the subject matter itself is not to be separated from the exegetical discussion. If, with someone's help, I learn to better understand the subject matter with which we both are concerned, and if I succeed in plausibly presenting this new understanding of the subject matter, this is a very strong sign that I have also understood the other person correctly and think within his meaning even where I go beyond his own notions, formulations, and arguments. The plausibility of my view of the subject matter that I have gained in the process of interpreting the thoughts of the other person speaks for the plausibility of the interpretation itself.

Naturally, there always remains as a certain limit the possibility that, moved by the thought of another person, I achieve a plausible view, but that with it I miss precisely that which the other person wanted to say. In other words, there remains the possibility of a so-called "fruitful misunderstanding." But who dares to say, and who has an unerring standard at his disposal to measure where in each case the legitimate further-thinking understanding stops and where the fruitful misunderstanding begins?

The exegetical discussion becomes somehow uninteresting and without substance if we artificially isolate the opinion of the interpreted author from the subject matter with which he and we are concerned, if both questions are not treated in one and the same breath. Such a combination of exegesis and discussion of the subject matter itself is, however, not an arbitrary and thoughtless mixing of things which are to be logically separated; rather, it corresponds to the particular logic of the dialogue.

That the exegetical consideration and the consideration of the subject matter itself interpenetrate to such an extent is also conditioned by the fact that it belongs to good dialogue to attempt so far as possible to make the arguments of the other persons "stronger." This is why the Platonic Socrates says I should try to take other men seriously and grant them a force of argumentation and meaning that perhaps they themselves have not even thought of.

4. All the affirmations of a dialogue partner are to be measured by and interpreted with respect to that which is ultimately at stake for him. Consequently, that which he says last is normally decisive and most important.

We often experience—with ourselves and with other people—that someone after long considerations (which are quite meaningful, in no way unclear and confused) finally declares: "What I actually wanted to say, is . . ." In other words, after steering toward a goal with various thoughts, he finally makes a special effort to come still closer to that aim than he had up to that point. It would be unjust to contend that in such a case the person in question, with all that he said before, had not yet really spoken to the subject matter. We can easily understand this phenomenon of conversation, if we take into account what has been mentioned before: namely, that notions and thoughts are "open to the subject matter itself." It is very well possible that we always speak to the subject matter, i.e., toward the subject matter, coming closer and closer, making it ever more precise, taking different viewpoints, clarifying, throwing out misunderstandings; and then, once again, we speak still more precisely to the subject matter, approach still more directly the subject matter of our dialogue itself with a formulation that, to be sure, still in no way "contains" the subject matter itself in final unambiguity. (Our thinking, our formulations, are probably prevented by their very essence from reaching such final unambiguity.)

From taking this state of affairs seriously there results what is also a quite obvious commandment of human decency: that one accepts such a final and precise statement of someone, that one lets be valid what someone wants to have uttered as his provisional last word about the subject matter, that accordingly one doesn't unnecessarily seek to force essential contradictions between that which someone said earlier and what was his final precise statement—that rather, one seeks, even if it may not be obvious at the first glance, to see the agreement between that which has been said previously and that which has been finally uttered, and to interpret the former with respect to the latter. Many merely verbalistic disputations could probably be avoided if one kept closer to this simple state of affairs, if one paid more attention to the general trend of a dialogue!

An implication of this last statement is that the rule we have exemplified with reference to brief conversations can also be applied to the interpretation of something of longer duration, even to the interpretation of the work of a whole lifetime. This means, again, for the interpretation of Dietrich Bonhoeffer, that we have to understand his whole theological work in the light of the theological motifs that finally, in the *Letters and Papers from Prison*,[2] became manifest. As far as I can see, during his life Bonhoeffer never took back anything of his former important utterances. Therefore, the later utterances (in the *Ethics*[3] and in *Letters and Papers from Prison*) gain a special weight for the interpretation of the total life work. The earlier utterances don't contradict, but rather must be interpreted in the light of these later trends. In this sense, I would like to speak of a "teleological interpretation" of Bonhoeffer's theological way of thinking, somewhat in the sense of Heidegger's statement: *Denken ist die Einschränkung auf einen Gedanken, der einst wie ein Stern am Himmel der Welt stehen bleibt.*[4] In this sense, we must keep in view the way as a whole; then we shall discover the traces and beginnings of the later developments already in the earlier writings. This is valid for Bonhoeffer to a very high degree. Thus, the longing for reality that breaks through in the *Letters and Papers from Prison* is to be observed from the outset, for instance, when in his doctoral thesis "Sanctorum Communio," written at the age of twenty, Bonhoeffer endeavored to grasp the Church of Christ simultaneously as both a theological and a sociological phenomenon.

5. A dialogue can be creative. A thought can be changed gradually in the course of a dialogue, so that finally something new results, which nonetheless was already there when the dialogue began.

So the notions and thoughts from which a dialogue is constructed have, as it were, a certain teleology toward a future form of affirmation and knowledge, a form that, at the end of the dialogue, may suddenly appear. However, the change, the creative process, is not the result of the inherent nature of these thoughts and notions, but rather of the encounter in dialogue with the subject matter concerning both partners. Dialogue exists precisely as this double encounter of the partners: in the dialogue with the subject matter and of their encounter with each other.

6. Because a dialogue is not to be understood as isolated in itself, but rather always as an encounter with the subject matter, occasionally it may be legitimate to lift a thought out of its context.

It may, for instance, occur that dialogue partners with vastly different and alien backgrounds of thought may only gradually approach each other, having a hard time understanding each other, although the phenomenon with reference to which they try to understand each other is one and the same. But it may then be that all at once one of them utters something that, while it is consistent with his background of thinking and fits into his system, nonetheless grants to both the sudden certainty that they have understood each other in regard to the subject matter. In this case the dialogue partner *A* will probably lift the particular utterance of *B* out of its context, which is for him alien and hard to understand, and he will for the time being hold to this affirmation alone. Perhaps, then, several statements of this kind will follow, from which will be built up a mutual understanding —a new knowledge, perhaps in a new terminology—in such a way, however, that a new system is formed of this understanding, a new system toward which the formerly heterogeneous systems of the two partners in the dialogue will be opened and relativised.

In this sense, for instance, we can take a few thoughts crucial to Pierre Teilhard de Chardin and, without regarding their

context of natural science, natural philosophy, and cosmologi-
cal eschatology, compare them with a few central thoughts
from the quite different kind of thought world of Dietrich Bonhoeffer, establishing a surprising accord in what, for instance,
concerns the universalistic understanding of Jesus Christ in
both of these thinkers, or, as another related example, in what
concerns the understanding of the worldliness of Christian existence.

These have been very simple observations concerning a
phenomenon that, without doubt, should be called a hermeneutical one. These are simple facts, which anybody can easily
verify. But perhaps the only really solid basis for all our deal-
ings with hermeneutics lies in the concrete, experienceable phenomenon.

There is still more to observe and to describe, for dialogue is life itself. We could, for instance, analyze what goes
on in the dialogical relationship between teacher and pupil,
between professor and student (insofar as this is an authentic
teacher-pupil relationship). It is probably not simply the case
that the teacher knows things while the student doesn't yet
know them.

But instead of continuing, let me close my remarks with
a general comment. We have limited our observations to
the reflective situation of a conscious and authentically disciplined dialogue, such as would occur in a scientific, philosophical, or theological discipline. However, even this kind
of dialogue flourishes, in the last analysis, out of elements
of a more original utterance, which nourish and steer the
reflection and at times appear in its course, as it were, as
erratic boulders. Dialogue, on the high hermeneutical level
of reflection, has its foundation in a more simple utterance
in a more elementary kind of personhood, which yet remains
dialogue and hermeneutical. But this more fundamental utterance would have to be the object of a more profound analysis
—no doubt a fascinating task!

The task of the historian "to establish how things actually
occurred" (according to Ranke's famous formulation), can

never and in any single case be accomplished completely. We certainly can establish that Caesar was assassinated in 44 B.C. But we shall never know completely what Caesar or Brutus or all the others experienced, thought, and felt at the time. Maybe they themselves didn't know clearly enough to formulate it. Yet this belongs to the reality of the *historical* event itself. There are no "brute facts"; there is only the mysterious, many-layered, always questionable total complex of man's historical experience. We certainly can make an agreement about the kind of abstractions, about the framework with whose help we will endeavor to record history. But historical reality itself nevertheless constantly transcends this framework and confronts us in overwhelming and fascinating strangeness. And if we want to deal with history, with reality itself, there is no other way left than to become aware of our own historicity, to "realize" it and again and again to venture into dialogue with history. This is the reason why we can say that dialogue is life itself.

NOTES

1. Martin Heidegger, *Unterwegs zur Sprache* (Pfullingen: Verlag Gunther Neske Pfullingen, 1959), pp. 97-98. "Hermeneutics in *Being and Time* means neither the doctrine about the art of interpretation, nor interpretation itself, but rather the attempt to determine the essence of interpretation first of all out of the hermeneutical."

2. London: SCM Press, 1953.

3. New York: Macmillan, 1955.

4. "Thinking is the being-restricted to one single thought, which, like a star, will remain in the heavens of the world."

II

**PHILOSOPHY AND
THE ART OF
INTERPRETATION**

Twofold always. May God us keep
From single vision, and Newton's sleep!
                    —WILLIAM BLAKE

✳ CONTEMPORARY PHILOSOPHY, like much theology, has as a central theme the problem of language. Linguistic analysts concentrate on the logic and use of language. Some neo-Kantians have stressed symbolic functions. Existential phenomenologists accent the descriptive and creative power of speaking. But whatever method the contemporary philosopher exercises, he grapples with some form of the problem of language.

In philosophy the issue of nonobjectifying discourse is hermeneutical. That is, the philosophical task is to elicit the principles informing interpretations of reality. The philosopher would guard others against unwitting uses of faulty presuppositions for interpretation. Also, he would guard himself against accepting a limiting method that interprets the meaning of interpretations by a "single vision." (Compare with Norman O. Brown's use of Blake's phrase in Chapter 1.)

In the chapters that follow, both Julián Marías and Owen Barfield direct their attention to keeping philosophy from "single vision and Newton's sleep," the modern Cartesian form of philosophical substantialism. Marías proposes a way to disclose presuppositions in philosophical interpretation by identifying basic metaphors. Barfield offers an explanation of poetic interpretation by focusing on the meaning of "inspiration." Thus,

37

the two contributors relate poetic and philosophic ways of thought in order to speak philosophically about the question at stake in this book: Under what principles does the art of interpretation proceed?

In his introduction to the first work by Ortega y Gasset, *Meditaciones del Quijote* (1957), Marías spoke to the question: "Concrete knowledge is *interpretation*, discovery of a *logos*, or meaning of things, based on a vital perspective." The vital perspective in philosophical meaning may be identified with the dynamic vision of imaginative literature. Marías could therefore write: "A theory is just another dramatic structure."

In "Philosophic Truth and the Metaphoric System" Marías appeals more to poetry than to drama for clarification of the philosophic enterprise. But the aim is the same as that of his earlier writing: infusing the art of philosophical interpretation with the power of creative imagination, i.e., seeing "an extremely close connection between metaphor and interpretation."

Barfield's aim is similar. Instead of using the poetic act as a means of interpreting philosophy, he applies philosophical understanding to an interpretation of the poetic act. He refers to poetry as a "crossing the threshold between two dimensions of consciousness." Poetry is a mode of cognition which demonstrates an aesthetic theory of knowledge. What was once called poetic inspiration from outside is called "the genius within," and the result of poetic inspiration ("the intuitive of the spiritual in man") is "a form of *knowledge*, but a *knowledge* that is to be won only *with the help* of imagination." Therefore, a philosophical understanding of imagination is basic to a method of interpretation, whether the interpretation is of poetry or philosophy.

Barfield intimates this in *Poetic Diction* (1928). There he argues against a nonaesthetic interpretation that operates exclusively under the strictures of the rational principle: "It can clear up obscurities, it can measure and enumerate with greater and ever greater precision, it can preserve us in the dignity and responsibility of our individual existences. But in no sense can it be said to *expand* consciousness. Only the poetic can do this: only poesy, pouring into language its creative intuitions, can preserve its living meaning and prevent it from crystallizing into a kind of algebra." The "expansion of consciousness" is important in interpretation because interpretation not only clarifies, but also creates, meaning. In *Poetic Diction*, therefore, Barfield emphasizes: "When we can experience a change of meaning—a *new* meaning—there we may really join hands and sing with the morning stars; for there we are in at the birth."

However, neither Barfield nor Marías indulges his poetic philosophizing to a romantic or idealistic excess. Marías denies the validity of aphoristic language for philosophy because it separates itself from other metaphors in a philosophic system; he holds that aphorisms are not amenable to justifications in the way that philosophic ideas must be. Barfield stops short of a pan-symbolism that might say: "the meaning of a poetic symbol can indeed be spoken of, but only in other poetic symbols." By excluding intentionally aphoristic and pan-symbolic modes of interpretation, the essays of Marías and Barfield may be contrasted with the one by Norman O. Brown. Thus, Marías and Barfield stand in the tradition of Plato and Kant, Coleridge and Ortega y Gasset, for whom the art of interpretation is a key to philosophical meaning when it is not radically ambiguous but precisely "twofold always."

3
Julián Marías:
Philosophic Truth
and the
Metaphoric System

ORTEGA Y GASSET frequently attended to the problem of metaphor, and, as a writer, he used metaphors widely. He believed that a metaphor is a means of making reality give reverberations. This has a close connection to the idea of truth, especially as interpreted by the Greeks under the name ἀλήθεια. I am going to start with this point of view, this theory of ἀλήθεια, because I think this is an important topic in recent philosophy, but a topic not always discussed clearly.

The Greek interpretation of truth as ἀλήθεια has been popular in philosophy since the publication by Martin Heidegger of *Sein und Zeit* in 1927. Heidegger concentrated on the etymological aspect of ἀλήθεια, from the ἀ— and λανθάνω, meaning "what is the hidden," "what is concealed." Also, there is some connection between ἀλήθιεα and λήθη, meaning "oblivion," "forgetfulness." In his definition Heidegger, therefore, insisted on the aspects of patency, manifestedness, *Unverborgenheit, Entbergung*, or unveilment of reality.

Since Heidegger's *Sein und Zeit*, this concept of ἀλήθιεα has become widely discussed in philosophy, but not many people know that Ortega y Gasset introduced this interpretation of ἀλήθεια in his first book, *Meditaciones del Quijote (Meditations on Quixote)*, in 1914. This was the nucleus of his interpreta-

tion of truth and reality in that work. But neither Heidegger nor
Ortega gave any indication of the sources of this etymological
interpretation. That is, both Heidegger and previously Ortega
used this interpretation philosophically, but they did not mention their sources for the etymological aspect of this idea of
truth.

It has been a bit difficult for me to find where this etymological interpretation first came from. I found that Nicolai
Hartmann in one of his early books, *Platos Logik des Seins*, in
1909, had insisted on this etymology of ἀλήθεια and had related
it to λήθης πηδίον, meaning "the field of oblivion," "of forgetfulness." Hartmann was especially interested in the negative
aspect of the concept of ἀλήθεια, the negative formal aspect of
this word, although the content of it is positive. But he did not
make any philosophical use of ἀλήθεια, and in the rest of his
works, he did not allude to the definition. His was merely an
etymological consideration.

I suspect the story of this interpretation of ἀλήθεια is older;
I suspect it dates at least to 1874. There is an interesting passage
in a rather forgotten German thinker, Gustav Teichmüller, who
in 1879 published a book, *Neue Studien zur Geschichte der
Begriffe*. He mentioned that Rassow had suggested a connection between λήθη and αληθής, and that in 1874 Walter, in *Die
Lehre der praktischen Vernunft in der griechischen Philosophie*,
had rejected the connection as a play of words, repulsive for the
philosophic consciousness. Teichmüller said, *"Während Rassow
die λήθη in etymologischer Verbindung mit αληθής stehend
glaubte, straft Walter (S. 448) sofort diesen 'für das philoso-
phische Bewusstsein wahrhaft degoutanten Wortwitz'."* He
believed that this might well be a play of words, but that it was
not *"degoutant."* Why? He said that *"Auch die Götter, sagt
Plato, lieben ja Scherz und Spiel. Hass und Abschen sind aber
keine guten Wegweiser der Interpretation."* Some fun is not
bad even for gods; and play is not bad for them either. Teichmüller was so interested in this possible connection between
λήθη and ἀληθής that he asked a colleague, a philologist named
Leo Meyer, who was a professor at Dorpat University, about the
linguistic connection. Leo Meyer gave him a note, which
Teichmüller published in his book. And this note, a purely

philological note, becomes the most complete account of the Greek meaning of ἀλήθεια and of the connections of this Greek word with all the motifs so interesting for the philosophy of the last decades. I think this is the origin of the etymological interpretation of ἀλήθεια.

But having noted these historical data, we still have not said anything especially important, because the important point is the meaning of ἀλήθεια. Ortega said that for the Greeks, truth is "discovery," "unveilment," "the removal of something which covers reality." Truth is manifestness; it is patency. Therefore, reality becomes really creative and not inertial *when we discover it*. Ortega said that "truth is always a new truth, because, after it is discovered, it has a kind of utilitarian layer which covers it and it loses its function as truth."

I think this notion of truth is important in connection with metaphor. First, it is important because ἀλήθεια means "discovery," "unveilment," *"Entbergung,"* "unconcealment." It is surprising that so important a concept as truth has a metaphorical name in the Greek language. And second, the function of ἀλήθεια, the function of truth, is very close to that of metaphor, because metaphor has the role of underlining certain aspects of reality, of making them shine. (By the way, this is the meaning of the word "argument," another important philosophical word. "To argue" is from the same root as *argentum*, ἀργυρός, "silver." Silver is the shining metal, the white metal. Therefore, *argumentum* would make something shining or white. We might say if silence is gold, philosophical argumentation is at least silver!) Thus, we see how metaphor is involved with the venerable and somehow adust philosophical word, "truth."

There are many, many such connections between philosophy and literature. There is, for example, a literary element in philosophical thought, at least inasmuch as philosophic thought has to discover that in reality some brilliance, some shining, is necessary in order to discover truth. That is, the power of discovery is closely connected with the capacity of making things "to shine." In addition, there are the philosophic forms, the literary forms of philosophy. Philosophy has had so many literary genres, some fortunate, some not so fortunate. The problem is that the content and the literary form used to express that content are extremely closely connected; hence, one cannot formulate just any type of philosophic thought in just any literary form. Writing a philosophical work has a certain destination, a certain claim upon the reader. What a pre-Socratic philosopher wanted to do when he wrote is entirely different from what an Idealist intended. And the Idealist's proposal is different still from the proposal of Aquinas, or Kant, or Hegel, or Wittgenstein.

There is also a third connection between philosophy and literature: the value of fiction as a mode of knowledge; and especially we may think of the novel in this regard. Unamuno or Kafka, or the existentialist thinkers like Gabriel Marcel or Jean-Paul Sartre, use fiction—both novels and plays—as a mode of knowledge. In 1938 I wrote an essay on Unamuno that was the point of departure for a book I later wrote on him. In that work I devoted a chapter to what I then called "the existential novel of Unamuno." (I don't think that there were existential novels *per se* then in world literature. They came a little later.) The novel is the detour Unamuno had to make in order to know human reality, human life and death, because he was an irrationalist, as most philosophers were in his time, and therefore he didn't believe that reason was adequate for knowing living reality, especially human life. He had to make a detour, a very fruitful one in his case, through imagination. Unamuno believed that the imagination is the most substantial of all human faculties. It is that which makes us penetrate the interior of other things, and especially of other persons; the only way to understand human life is to attend to it, that is, to follow it in its temporality by means of narration and especially in the novel. Therefore, the novel becomes a mode of knowledge or interpretation of human life.

Then there is metaphor itself. Metaphor has been widely used in literature, especially in poetry; and there are many very interesting theories about the use of metaphor in poetry. But metaphor is also a mental tool, that is, a means of knowing the reality which can be known in no other way. The problem is this: if a philosopher discovers a *new* reality, or at least a *new* aspect of reality, there will be no name for it. Therefore, the problem of naming *new* realities, or *new* aspects of reality, is the same for a philosopher as for an explorer when he discovers a new continent or a new island. There are no names. He cannot consult the map. All discoverers have to give names. Sometimes they give old names, for instance, names from their old country, English names in North America, or Spanish names in Mexico and in South America, or in this country, too. Sometimes they add the word "new" to the old name, as in "New York," "New London," etc.

This is more or less the same as the situation of the philosopher who is trying to name new realities. He can just invent a name, a brand-new name, a "term," a neologism. But a name or word generally is something that exists prior to our experience of the thing the word names. It is a social reality that precedes all of us, and this is why we understand it. We can use it, and we understand it because it precedes us. But if I now invent a word it is not really a word; you do not understand it. I have to explain it. I have to explain that I give a certain meaning to the word I just invented. It is not a proper word, it is a "term." A "term" is a word (or a nonword) that has to be defined. Therefore the similarity between words and terms is a very superficial one. Neologisms (the words invented to name things) are very dangerous. First of all, most of the time they are literary failures. A literary page full of neologisms gives a strange impression. On the other hand, they are dangerous because they may produce an illusion, that of being reality when only being "terms."

The danger here can be expressed by an example from the medical jargon that most doctors use. If I have a very bad headache, I consult my doctor and he will say, "Oh, well, yes, you have cephalalgia." Well, this is exactly what I already knew, only he said it in Greek. The doctor knows a little more terminology than I. But what about the reality of my headache? This is the trouble with neologisms. And philosophy, when it is inclined to use neologisms, becomes a kind of scholasticism. Scholasticism, in this very general way, is a philosophical position that comes from a tradition closely linked to a terminology. The "scholastic" philosopher too often just operates with terms and combines them instead of looking at things. (There are two ways of philosophizing: the one is to combine terms, and the other is to look at things. I am always afraid of nonvisual philosophy.)

There is another way of naming new realities: using old words. But this is not adequate, because the realities are really new, and therefore the name does not really name them. You can say "New York," but "New York" is more or less a metaphor. It is an old word used obliquely and with a different meaning. The metaphorical usage of a word suggests that the meaning is not exactly what is said, but something different. Therefore, the role of the metaphor is like my finger when I point to something. When I point to something, I am suggesting that you look in this direction in order to discover what I am seeing. I am not suggesting you look at my finger. Some people do. And this is very surprising. Unfortunately this also happens in philosophy!

Yet the role of metaphor in poetry and in philosophy is somehow different. Metaphor is μεταφορά, a "transposition," or a "translation." It is important in using metaphors that the previous meaning of the word is not lost. When it is lost there is no metaphor at all. For instance, the word "money" comes from the word *moneta*. Moneta was the place in Rome where there was a temple, the temple of Juno Moneta. And this is where the Roman mint was located. Therefore, "money" comes from *moneta*, which becomes *moneda*, "coin," in Spanish, or *monnaie* in French. But we have forgotten this connection. When we say *moneda* in Spanish or *money* in English, we don't think of Juno Moneta. It is entirely forgotten, and therefore the word is no longer a metaphor. Another example of this phenomenon is the French word for "strike"—*grève*. *Grève* is a place in Paris where unemployed workers used to meet, and *etre ên grève* meant "to be unemployed." But in France none now knows this meaning of the word *grève*, and therefore it is not a metaphorical word. Again, if I speak of the rose cheeks of a girl, they do not become roses, fortunately. Yet they have *something* to do with roses and therefore there is a suggestion that they are *like* roses. In old Sanskrit poetry, most comparisons were introduced not by "like" but by a negation. For instance, today one might say, "the King is loving like a father." In Sanskrit it would be, "the King is loving, not a father." That is, this metaphor is at the same time an affirmation and a negation. So with or without the term "like," in poetry we have an inaccurate identification between two terms of a comparison, and the poetic value consists in this abusive and exaggerated identification. This is the poetic usage of metaphor.

In philosophy it is different; the philosopher has an ironical view of metaphor. That is, the identification is not to be taken seriously, and we know it. Therefore, whereas the poetic metaphor is the elementary aesthetic object (Ortega called it "the cell of beauty"), the philosophic metaphor is something that is said in *modo obliquo*, without insisting too much on it, without intending it literally. The philosophic metaphor suggests that we follow a certain line of thought so we can discover what is intended. In philosophy, metaphor is a mode of discovery.

But philosophy not only discovers, it also interprets. And interpreting reality seems to imply that there is a reality out there and that we may make a particular operation with that reality that will be called "interpretation." This is not entirely the case, because what we call reality is just an interpretation. We perceive reality, and we give it names, and we use it for many purposes. We live with it as if it were something previously interpreted. For instance, I am now writing this essay, and I take its subject matter to be something on which one can write. You may be sitting on a chair while reading this book, but you may do so only if you have a previous interpretation of what you are sitting on to be a "chair." And if I drink a little water, I interpret water to be a drink, but when I wash my hands, I interpret water in a very different way, and if I swim, I interpret it again in a third way, and if I want to put out fire with water, it is again a new interpretation. Therefore, things have been shown to me since I was born in many different interpretations. They are interpreted for me by my parents, my friends, teachers and the society. I am given *social* interpretations prior to any particular activity of mine. So if we now should hear thunder, we would call it an electric phenomenon because we are living in the country of Benjamin Franklin in the twentieth century; but a Roman would have said that

Jupiter is angry, and in still another society they would say it is an omen. Therefore, there is an interpretative character to reality that belongs to it as such. And far from our adding interpretations to reality, the great question in philosophy is to remove interpretations. That is, we have to remove interpretations if we want to reach the "naked reality," if this were possible.

Therefore I believe that the universe is covered by a patina of interpretations, and most of these interpretations are metaphors. Only we tend to forget this. When we say, for instance, "Orient," we no longer think of a place where things are born; but this is what "Orient" means, being taken from the Latin verb *orior, ortus,* "to be born." We forget this interpretation of the word Orient and use it as a simple, normal word of the language, or as a "term." Interpretations, then, are the *real* world we live in. One of the tasks of philosophy is to remove these interpretations in order to get at the "naked reality." The trouble is that reality is very much like an onion, or an artichoke. If I remove a leaf, an interpretation, there is another, and a second, and a third. And if I proceed to remove all interpretations, the rest is nothing. Does this mean that reality is nothing at all, just interpretations? By no means. Reality is something that makes me make interpretations. That is, I have to make interpretations of some reality, but I never can reach the reality without any interpretations. As a philosopher, I have to pierce through the whole history of interpretations in historical order, but in reverse, starting from the present and going back to primitive man.

Thus we see that there is an extremely close connection between metaphor and interpretation, since most interpretations are metaphoric. Look, for instance, at something so serious as international politics. We have lived since 1945 with two metaphors, two very modest poetic metaphors: Iron Curtain and Cold War. We speak of the Iron Curtain as if it were a reality. We speak of the Cold War and we are afraid it will get warmer. There are many books on these metaphors. They have become the most powerful "realities" in this world, yet they are metaphors, very basic metaphors. Just think of the possibilities if these two metaphors did not exist.

There are two different possibilities: the first is that there would be no such metaphors. If this were the case, I would be more afraid than I already am, because having these metaphors, we may deal with the very dangerous realities that they name and interpret. And as long as we have a name for them, we can somehow control them. The second possibility is that the metaphor would be different, that instead of speaking of Iron Curtain as Winston Churchill did or of Cold War some other metaphors would be used. In this latter case, I am sure international policies would be different, because we would then have a different interpretation of the threat of these realities, and the ways to deal with them would have to be altered accordingly. I am sure that the wall of Berlin would never have been built if the metaphor Iron Curtain had not been used, because this is just a realization of that metaphor. The concrete wall in Berlin is a literal counterpart to the metaphor.

We can say, then, that the universe is built on metaphors, that metaphors are the foundation of everyday reality, and that when we believe we walk on earth, we really walk on metaphors. And the greatest metaphor of all is "being." "Being" is an interpretation of reality. It is the most famous and illustrious interpretation of reality. The all-important verb "to be" is not really a verb. In English you say, "I *am*," "He *is*," and "I *was*"; but you also say "to *be*." "Am," "is," "was," "be"—they don't fit together. They are independent words, independent pieces of words that are gathered together at the end of improvisation. The same thing happens in Spanish and in French and in Latin, of course, where these others come from; and in Greek and, I think, in all languages. "To be" is not an elementary verb, but something composed of many independent words that came to the rescue when men needed this little word "to be."

"Being" is an interpretation of reality, and reality is simply what I constantly find around me before any interpretation. To say that something *is* means that it has some consistency. If I say *A* is *B*, I presuppose that when I am saying *B*, *A* is still *A*. But imagine that reality is changing, continuously changing, that it has no fixity. In that case I could not say *A* is *B*, because when I am uttering the word *B*, *A* would no longer be *A*.

Therefore, to use the metaphor "being" implies a presupposition, a previous interpretation of reality as something that is. The word ὄν in Parmenides means just this consistency. Things *consist* of something: of having the "being" of dogs or horses or sheep, trees or water, earth or fire, cold or hot, or blue, or anything. But Parmenides discovered that things simply consist of consisting; they consist of consistency, and this is the meaning of the word ὄν. But if I ask a question about "being," if I ask what "being" is, I already assume that there is "being." Therefore there is a pretheoretical belief in "being" before the philosophical and theological question about being is posed. The Aristotelian question (τί τὸ ὄν;) is not a first question. It is not a radical question in philosophy, because it already presupposes the belief in "being," the belief in ὄν, or consistency. This is the principal philosophic instance of the fact that reality is covered by a layer of interpretations, most of them metaphoric.

The role of philosophy, as we have said, is to remove these interpretations, to unveil reality, to unconceal and discover the reality lying under these interpretations. This is the meaning of the word *apocalypsis* (ἀποκαλύψις), "to get rid of a veil that covers things." There is an interesting little line from Critias; it is interesting because in a single line we find all the Greek words for the notions we are considering here. In a satirical drama, *Sisyphos,* Critias explains the origin of the belief in gods, using in the same line the four essential words, ψεῦδος, καλύπτειν ἀλήθεια and λόγος. The line reads: ψευδεῖ καλύψας τὴν ἀλήθειαν λόγωι. Kathleen Freeman translated this line: "Covering up the truth with a false theory." Similarly in a poem by Parmenides, the ἡλιάδες κοῦραι, we read:

> ἡλιάδες κοῦραι, προλιποῦσαι δώματα Νυκτός,
> εἰς φάος, ὠσάμεναι κράτων ἄπο χερσὶ καλύπτρας.

Here is the same idea of unveiling, of removing the veils with the hands; discovery is the getting rid of a veil that covered reality. This is ἀλήθεια, and again ἀποκαλύψις, this latter being a more expressive and active word.

Having indicated the connection between philosophic truth and metaphor I would like to call attention to some of the greatest metaphors in philosophic thought. Ortega wrote an essay in 1924 whose title was "The Two Great Metaphors." But in 1916, a few years before this essay, he had given a course in Buenos Aires. One of the lessons in this course had a title "The Three Great Metaphors." In 1916, there were three; in 1924, there were just two. The discrepancy lies in the fact that in the later work he did not deal with the third, which was his own metaphor. He did not want to publish anything about this, and the text therefore waited till his death for publication.

The first metaphor is a metaphor of Greece and of the Middle Ages: the interpretation of consciousness in Greek philosophy and in medieval philosophy. The metaphor comes from the idea of the ἐκμαγεῖον, of the wax table and the stamp. It is taken from the way the Greeks and Romans wrote on wax tablets with a stylus. You may find this great metaphor in Plato's *Theaetetus* and again in Aristotle's *De Anima*. The whole of medieval philosophy is filled with this metaphor of *consciousness as an impression*. Therefore in ancient and medieval philosophy the phenomenon of knowledge is interpreted as the trace of something imprinted on a wax tablet. The metaphor implies the presupposition of two *independent* things: the wax and the stamp. But philosophers came to challenge this presupposition.

After the Renaissance, especially after Descartes, another metaphor was used. This is that of the container and the content. Philosophers began to speak of the contents of consciousness, and this produced Idealism. Reality as such, material reality, was conceived to be a content of consciousness, something enveloped in my consciousness. Therefore, consciousness is creation. If the Realistic philosophy of Greece and the Middle Ages was supported by one basic metaphor, the modern philosophy of Idealism was supported by another.

But Ortega suggested still a third metaphor: a metaphor that would view the subject and the object as facing one another and inseparable. The image he used is that of the *dii consentes*, the gods, like Castor and Pollux, who lived together. Instead of the imprint on the wax, instead of the contents of consciousness, there is implied two irreducible realities facing each other, irreducible and inseparable, subject and object, or "I and circumstance," as he preferred to say. Again, Ortega put this whole notion metaphorically in the title of an essay where he included a glimpse into his whole philosophic system; the title was "Adam in Paradise." "Adam in Paradise" is another metaphoric way of saying "I and my circumstance."

We could summarize briefly the whole history of philosophy in three metaphors. As long as we remain inside one of them, our interpretation of reality will be conditioned by a single metaphor, a metaphor so elementary and so simple that we are not usually aware of it. Greek and medieval philosophers spoke of the *tabula rasa*, or the idea of *intellectus* as *tabula rasa in qua nil scriptum est;* modern idealistic philosophers spoke of the contents of consciousness, of reality as being merely ideas. These ways of speaking were metaphorical. And now we have a third metaphor, which may last a long time, or perhaps not, but which will one day certainly be replaced by another metaphor, a fourth metaphor.

This leads, finally, to some observations about the concrete character of metaphors. Metaphors are not independent; they may not be viewed in isolation. They throw light on reality, and they discover certain aspects of reality. But there is always a plurality of aspects. Dilthey said, "*Leben ist eben mehrseitig*" (Life is many-sided). Reality, therefore, exists in a perspectival way. Any reality has to be considered from a certain point of view. But the perspective is not alien and foreign to reality; it is an intrinsic moment of it, that is, a perspective is an ingredient or element of reality so that reality constitutes itself in a perspective. Reality is linked to a point of view and therefore to an aspect. But since reality has many aspects, the metaphor that discovers one aspect is connected with other metaphors, which are not independent, but are implicated by the previous metaphor. A central metaphor integrates itself with other complementary metaphors, which in turn discover other connected aspects of reality. Therefore, the metaphoric approach to reality utilized by the philosopher is a never-ending process. Thinking cannot stop. The imperative of thinking is to keep thinking; the imperative of a vision is to keep looking at things.

There is an interconnection between philosophic metaphors that illuminate each other. And this is what I call the metaphoric system: metaphors that are linked together, and that illuminate the different faces of reality. Metaphors that explore and discover the many sides of reality are interconnected; they are a system that is the correlation of philosophic truth as discovery, as ἀλήθεια. The only way to discover reality is *to transit*, to go through it, to follow it. We can only make the discovery of reality by following the intricacy of its interpretations, which are metaphorical.

One can speak of an original metaphor whose role is not to include the whole interpretation of reality in it; it is simply impossible that a single sentence can unveil all reality. The systematic character of reality makes impossible any kind of total formula. This is why an aphorism is a false way of philosophic expression: an aphorism is something that is cut off from the root; it is artificially independent, and consists of the elimination of its real connections. When I utter an aphorism I never say why I think what I am saying, or what is the justification of what I am saying. Therefore an aphorism, even if it is true, is philosophically false, because it is unjustified in itself; and philosophy is justification. I could call philosophy "the justified vision." *Thinking* cannot proceed aphoristically. I can limit myself to a single metaphor, but no formula can give me the secret of reality. The role of the central or original metaphor is simply to trigger (the French would say *déclancher*) the whole set of connected metaphors that come to mind so I can follow the whole series of them into reality as such.

Such is the central metaphor of a philosophic system: the "Idea" (εἶδος, ἰδέα) in Plato or the concept of ὀνσία in Aristotle; the *cogito* in Descartes, or the metaphoric concept of *monad* in Leibniz; the idea of the *Absolute* in Hegel, or the principle, "I and my circumstance," in Ortega. But none of these men's systems can be *identified* with these formulas. These formulas can only trigger the active development of the metaphoric system, which, in its turn, allows me to penetrate reality and to follow the real intricacies of it. I would suggest, therefore, that when again you read a philosopher's book, you try to discover the hidden metaphor that lies under the truth of the philosophic system, and try to bring it to light.

4
Owen Barfield:
Imagination and
Inspiration

I WANT TO START by drawing your attention to something that stands at the very beginning of perhaps the greatest of all the documents that have come down to us from the literature of the ancient East. I mean the "Divine Song" as it is called: the *Bhagavad-Gita*. You will all, I am sure, have read it, and you will recall how the scene is set at the opening. Two hostile armies are drawn up in battle array and the fighting is about to begin. But in the moment of extreme tension the warrior-prince Arjuna bids his charioteer drive him to a position between the two armies in order that they may talk for a little. It is done, and Arjuna, who is greatly troubled in his soul, reveals to the charioteer the source of his perplexity and his misery. It is in the nature of a civil war, where kinsman is ranged against kinsman and, for that and other reasons, Arjuna finds in himself no desire to fight. It is not because he is afraid. "I do not wish to kill," he says, "though they kill me." Looking ahead, he sees only evils of all kinds coming of the battle. Families will be disintegrated. All sorts of impiety will become rife. The enemy are criminals or tyrants, and yet if he kills them, he will incur sin. "I do not wish for victory, nor sovereignty, nor pleasures, nor even life." Having finished his long speech, Arjuna casts aside his bow and sits down in his chariot overcome by grief.

The charioteer is Krishna, an avatar of the Deity himself; and the song, as you know, consists of the dialogue that ensues between the man and the God. Krishna's immediate response to Arjuna amounts to an endeavor to transpose the thinking of Arjuna to another level or plane of consciousness altogether—to a fresh dimension, within which all the objections he has raised are irrelevant, because unreal or superseded. The wise grieve neither for the living nor the dead. "Never did I not exist, nor you, nor these princes; nor will any one of us ever hereafter cease to be. . . . There is no existence for that which is unreal; there is no nonexistence for that which is real." So Krishna argues, saying in effect that the true, the real self of Arjuna—as well as that of those he will be killing—is to be found only in an imperishable realm beyond action and beyond expression. "He who thinks one to be the killer and he who thinks one to be the killed, both know nothing. He kills not, is not killed. He is not born, nor does he ever die . . ." and so on. *"Therefore,"* says Krishna—and now there comes what is perhaps for most Western readers, on a first reading, a dramatic surprise, if not a rude shock. It shocked Thoreau, and later on it shocked Gandhi. Krishna has raised the discourse, one could say, to the level of the Absolute; he is endeavoring to make Arjuna see it from that perspective. It is a point of view from which the coming battle is irrelevant, because the whole of the world as we know it from the everyday point of view is an unreality, an illusion, a mere catenation of appearances. *"Therefore,"* he goes on—but he does not go on to say, as we rather expect: "Therefore withdraw from the battle and from the world and cultivate reality, cultivate the Absolute, cultivate the inexpressible." On the contrary, he utters the surprising conclusion: *"Therefore fight on!"* [1]

There are three prominent features that I want to stress here. First, that the main purpose of the *Gita* is, clearly, to raise the thinking, or the consciousness of the protagonist, Arjuna, from the ordinary plane to a higher one, or into another dimension, to which quite different rules apply; secondly, the means by which this is accomplished is a communication and a revelation made by a spirit-being who already lives on that other plane, in this case a temporarily incarnate one: that is, the God Krishna himself; and thirdly, that we are told not to draw conclusions for the lower plane from the higher one, to which the ordinary logical categories do not apply. Whatever we, or others, do or leave undone is from that higher plane or point of view unreal or unimportant; but we are *not*, from this, to conclude, for instance, with the complacent Frenchman: "*Tout comprendre c'est pardonner*," to endorse the papers "No action required" and file them away. On the contrary, we are to behave in exactly the opposite way. We are to follow the rules applicable to the lower plane, the ordinary dimension.

And note particularly, before we leave the *Bhagavad-Gita*, the change of atmosphere that immediately precedes, and then accompanies, that moment of vision or of direct experience that occurs later in the poem. In the *argument* Krishna has merely indicated the existence of this higher plane of consciousness. Later he raises Arjuna to an actual experience of it. He does this by revealing Himself in his universal, divine nature:

> The great Lord then showed to the son of Pritha his supreme divine form, having many mouths and eyes. . . . If in the heavens, the lustre of a thousand suns burst forth all at once, that would be like the lustre of that mighty one. There the son of Pandu beheld in the body of the God of Gods the whole universe all in one and divided into numerous divisions.[2]

It is indeed another dimension of consciousness—a fundamentally inexpressible one (how inadequate, for instance, is that quantitative reference to "many mouths and eyes"!) and Arjuna shows his numinous awareness of the transition. We are told that his hair stood on end and "he bowed his head before the God, and spoke with joined hands."

There are then two different planes of consciousness with what I will call a "threshold" between them. The poem does not say that the threshold is one that can never be crossed. On the contrary, it is essentially the story of Arjuna's being led across it by Krishna. What the poem does inculcate is that, though it may be crossed, it does not cease for that reason to exist. It must not be forgotten; it must not be left out of account. The two opposite sides of the threshold must never be confused with one another. If they are, the result will be only a worse disorder.

And now I will ask you to put the *Bhagavad-Gita,* and everything to do with Buddhism and the whole oriental tradition out of your minds for a time, and to bring before them instead a much later utterance of a very different nature. I am referring to the verse from William Blake's poem, which he included in a letter to his friend Thomas Butts, and in which he stresses that his own "vision" is always a "double" one. It may be more than double, but it is never less. It is:

> Twofold always. May God us keep
> From single vision, and Newton's sleep! [3]

You will be surprised, perhaps a little annoyed, when, having quoted this couplet from Blake, with its emphatic distinction between the kind of vision that is only "single" and the kind that is "twofold" or "double," I *again* call on you to leave Blake behind altogether, while I again go on to speak of something quite different. It is my hope that the spasmodic, or at all events disjointed, beginning of this essay will be mended and justified before it reaches its conclusion.

In the fall of this year I listened to a lecture given to the graduates of Brandeis University by a professor from the Department of Electrical Engineering at M.I.T. His more recent researches had been directed to the theory of optics and the neurology of perception; but he had also, at some stage in his career, practiced as a psychiatrist. He told us that he was much troubled about the behavior of neurons; and more particularly by the kind of intercommunication that appears to go on between them, which he said is both "direct" and "universal." He went on to say that his own science of neurophysiology was in a most unsatisfactory state, and he compared it unfavorably with the science of physics. The physicist had something he could teach; but he, as a neurophysiologist, had literally noth-

ing he could teach—indeed, it was because of this difficulty
that he found himself addressing a humanities department, in
the vague hope that he might get some useful comment from
them. The trouble was, what he called the "mind-body" problem. Physics had come up against this problem, also, but only
at a late stage in its development—only now—so that the long
history that had led up to it could at least be usefully taught and
learned. But neurophysiology came up against this same problem at the very outset. One neuron incorporates the mind-body
problem as inexorably as the whole system does; and it is a
problem to which no answer has even begun to be found. The
problem is that no satisfactory transition has been achieved from
a context in which you are talking about what is called "matter"
to a context in which you are talking about "mind." He threw
out a number of suggestions—conclusions he had felt tentatively
inclined to adopt, but in which he felt no confidence. Perhaps,
after all, "neuron" is only a kind of word. Perhaps we ought to
think of it as a "point of view" rather than as an object. Should
we assume that there are two kinds of science: (1) the ordinary
one, and (2) a science that is more like an art, where you find
out about what you are doing by doing it, rather than by thinking about it? And so on. I should add that, towards the conclusion of his lecture, he told us that, because of its total failure
before this problem, he considered that the science of psychology (at all events the psychology of perception) had made
no progress whatever in the last hundred years. It had been
dead since 1864, the date of Helmholtz's work on optics; and
the science of physiology had been equally dead since 1877.
Finally, he confided in us that he had been chuckling a good
deal to observe his colleagues in the biology department labori-
ously reaching the same foregone checkmate in their researches
into genes and chromosomes.

Now, of course, all this is only a particular example, though
I found it a striking one, of something the wide-awake have
been aware of for a long time. I mean the existence, in the whole
structure of Western thought, of an impassable barrier between
what we call "mind" (or what we in fact think of as "mind,"
whether we call it by that name or by some other) and what we

call, or what we in fact think of, as "matter." It remains a barrier that is only masked by determined attempts to ignore it, and that is again masked, but not penetrated, by the invention and use of portmanteau terms like "psychosomatic."

The first question I want to raise, then, is this: is there any connection between this impassable barrier that we are familiar with today and that "threshold" between two planes or dimensions of consciousness on which, as we saw, the message of the *Bhagavad-Gita* and much of the traditional wisdom of the East is based? My own conviction is that the connection is a close one, though it can only be traced historically. In other words, although it would be superficial and indeed inaccurate to identify the one unreflectively with the other, it would not be difficult to show, as a matter of historical development, how the later has grown up out of the earlier.

It would not be difficult, but it would be quite a long business. For instance, the *Bhagavad-Gita* was concerned with the threshold between the self on the one hand and what is ordinarily regarded as "not-self" on the other. But the barrier between mind and matter, in the form in which it has been a problem for natural science, is not obviously identical with this, though it may remind us of it. Tracing historically the mind-body problem with which my M.I.T. professor was so concerned, we are led back not (or not immediately) to the ancient civilizations of the Far East, but rather to the origins of Greek philosophy. And the Greek philosophers did not begin by formulating the problem in terms of a dichotomy between self and not-self. I believe it was not until the time of the later Stoics that there were expressions and ideas for the translating of which we should need to pray in aid such terms as "subject" and "object." What they were concerned about was the apparently unresolvable cleavage between other pairs of opposites, pairs such as "being" and "becoming," "rest" and "motion," "one" and "many." It was through this line of investigation, culminating in Aristotle's treatment of it, that they succeeded in establishing the principle of identity, and of mutually exclusive identities, on which the subsequent thought and life of the West has been based. It was through this line of investigation and this way of thought that a clear distinction between mind and matter first came about.

But we should be careful to note that throughout this time, and for many centuries after the Schools of Philosophy were closed by Justinian—that throughout the whole of the Middle Ages the logic that is based on the psychology of mutually exclusive identities (and that is therefore so closely involved with the self's awareness of its own identity) was by no means coincident with a distinction between mind and matter. To realize this, one has only to think of Aquinas's elaborate angelology, which is closely integrated with his whole psychological theory, while, in the unphilosophical world of general cultural life, the popularity of the allegorical vision as a literary form, as well as a large number of other features, testify to the fact that what you got, so to speak, when you had eliminated matter from your considerations, was not the bare isolated self, the pure subject, to which all else that was real was counterposed as object, but something like a nonmaterial world in which the self had its place along with other selves, incarnate or discarnate, other nonmaterial beings, forces, influences, with which the self was in direct and universal communication.

Moreover, all this nonmaterial "other" (if I may lump together in this inelegant expression all that was conceived as nonmaterial, but also as not-self) was not necessarily limited in its operations either to the individual psyche of the person concerned or even to his own particular physical body. It included the hierarchy of imperceptible beings that constituted the process of nature itself at the prematerial stages of that process. If *natura naturata* was only accessible through sense-perception, there were other channels of communication between the self and *natura naturans*. It was of course on this whole conception that the highly inaccurate sciences of astrology, alchemy, medieval physiology, medicine, and so forth were largely based.

I do not perhaps need to remind you that natural science as we know it—the science that dates back to the scientific revolution and no further—is based above all on one important modification of scientific method. It is that modification which brought it about that what we called "occult qualities" are by definition, or at least by way of axiom, to be altogether excluded from the field of scientific inquiry. But of course all that I have just been speaking of, all that can be called *natura naturans* as distinct from *natura naturata*, all that is not either objectively observable "matter" on the one hand, or simply the observer himself perceiving and thinking on the other, comes under the heading of "occult qualities." And so we reach the dichotomy that was formulated by Descartes, according to which all that is not a human self is matter; and by the time the scientific revolution was accomplished, our Western distinction between mind and matter had come, by its own route, to coincide with that much older Eastern one of self from not-self.

You get, in other words, a new awareness, and a greatly enhanced one, of that threshold before which, when he was invited to cross it, Arjuna experienced such overwhelming terror that every hair of his head stood on end. And I believe *our* terror at the thought of being called on to cross it is no less than his. Indeed, I would say it is greater. Only in our case it is disguised from us—or rather its very intensity has led us to conceal its true nature from ourselves. Something of this terror I detect, for instance, in the emotional overtones that accompanied the rejection of the so-called "occult qualities" from the field of scientific inquiry and which still often accompany any reference to them. It is a commonplace that violent hatred generally has fear somewhere beneath it.

But, rather than expatiating on this, let me try to record some of the responses this new and sharper awareness of an impassable threshold between self and not-self has evoked in Western thought. I have three particular ones in mind.

The first is the simple one with which we are all familiar. It is that view of the world that divides, more sharply than anything else does, the fundamental outlook of the West from the fundamental attitude of the East; and it amounts to a denial that the threshold is a threshold at all. This is perhaps more often an implicit rather than an explicit conviction, and it has been well summed up in the maxim: *De non apparentibus et non existentibus eadem est ratio* (the nonphenomenal is the nonexistent). Coleridge sometimes called it "the despotism of the eye."

On this view what I have been calling a "threshold" between two dimensions or planes of consciousness is not a threshold but a terminus. It is the edge of things. If it can be called a boundary at all, it is the boundary between existence and nothing. This was the response of the whole of natural science down to the end of the nineteenth century; it is still the working assumption of most scientists and of course of popular scientism. It does not make much difference whether you call it materialism, or positivism, or by some other name. Followed to its logical conclusion, it will be found to involve denying the existence of the self also. (It is not often thought through so clearly; but I feel the corollary should be mentioned, though it cannot here be pursued.)

In the realm of literature and criticism perhaps the most notable manifestation of this one of my three responses has been the critical theory of I. A. Richards,[4] based on a dichotomy between referential language on the one hand, that is propositions *de apparentibus*, and on the other hand the emotive language, which is all we are in fact uttering when we purport to be propounding *de non apparentibus*.

Before I go on to my second response, I must say something of a further development that took place in the status of what I am calling the "threshold." It is as if more and more matters were being drawn into its sphere of influence, to be split between one side of it and the other. We have seen how the threshold between mind and matter has become also a threshold between self and not-self. With the coming of Immanuel Kant and the almost universal acceptance of Kantianism it becomes, in addition, a threshold between two more pairs of opposites: namely the knowable and the unknowable. From one point of view this represents a fortifying and strengthening of the barrier, since that becomes in theory even more impassable. But note, on the other hand, that acceptance of Kantianism also rules out the first response. For those who accept it, Kantianism reinstates the threshold as being in fact a threshold, that is a boundary, between two worlds and not simply the terminus of the only world there is. As far as science is concerned, this perhaps made little difference—though it was otherwise with the *philosophy* of science, so far as there is one—because for the practicing scientist the distinction between the unknowable and the nonexistent is not important. In philosophy it led to the whole not ignoble development of subjective idealism. In literature and art and criticism I seem to detect, as the result of this further modification of the threshold, what I can only call the mood of withdrawal, irony, sometimes defeatism, which has enthralled the culture of the West for the last hundred years or so—the kind of romanticism, for instance, that is called "negative," an ironical acceptance of human limitations being substituted for any endeavour to expand them.

To one or other of the two responses I have outlined I suppose we also owe, in the realm of theology, the rise of ethical secularism, and more lately, its modified form of the demythologizing principle. Myths all sprang from the illusion that the threshold can be crossed by the human mind, or could at one time be so crossed. But the threshold is in fact immutable and eternal, so the myths must be scrapped. So runs the tale. It only remains to add, as touching these first two responses, that both of them also lead inevitably to the scientific *impasse* I referred to some while back, that is, the intractableness of what my lecturer called "the mind-body problem." The difficulty here is that it is not simply scientific theory, but the scientific *method* itself that rules out any approach to the problem. It cannot be otherwise, so long as that method continues to assume as given the proposition: *De non apparentibus et non existentibus eadem est ratio*.

I come, then, to the third response, and with that to the real subject of my essay. For there has been yet another alteration in the status of the threshold, and one which is characteristic most of all of our own day, though it began to show itself here and there many years ago. And what I have in mind now is a growing suspicion—at first no more than a suspicion, a hint here, a speculation there, an actual discovery somewhere else— all of which go to suggest that this threshold is not after all so utterly impassable as we in the West had been led to suppose.

It seems to me that quite a number of events, or developments, have joined together in bringing about this last alteration, but I shall mention only three of them. The order in which I have placed them is not significant. The first was the reluctant recognition by the Western intellect that mind and consciousness are not synonymous; that there is a realm, or a sphere, or a mode of being, or a dimension, in which events and activities occur that can only be classified as "mental," notwithstanding the fact that they are unconscious. (It will be recalled that, on a strictly Cartesian view, anything which is not self-conscious must be classified as "matter.") We associate this development with the name of Freud, and it is Freud who has made "the unconscious" a household word. But the admission was forced from us before Freud was born, when even so staunch a positivist as Herbert Spencer was obliged to concede that: "Mysterious as seems the consciousness of something which is yet out of consciousness, we are obliged to think it." Incidentally this mysterious category (a consciousness of which we are not conscious) had formed an integral part of Coleridge's concepts of *genius* and of *imagination* and of the fundamental distinction he divined between the *understanding* and the *reason*, of which I shall have a little more to say at the conclusion of this essay. Coleridge's positive intuition was largely ignored; but the hesitating admission of the same truth that was afterwards forced on an honest Victorian intellect by the facts of life, has of course grown in our time to a general acceptance, one could say a taking-for-granted, that there is a dimension of mind, a reaction to experience that we can only describe in terms of conscious mind, but that is sharply cut off from our self-consciousness and yet is not entirely irrelevant to it. It is a realm that is governed by quite different laws from those which we recognize and obey in our conscious waking lives. There is a threshold between the two worlds, but we cross it in sleep, and in our remembered dreams we even bring back, though usually in an unintelligible form, something of the goings on upon that further side of it. That the being called man spends about one-third of his time asleep is a fact that for centuries had been simply ignored by Western philosophy and psychology, though the business of that philosophy and especially of that psychology had been to determine the nature of man. Now at last that omission has been, in a measure, rectified.

The second event was itself a kind of crossing of a threshold—a threshold that had existed and remained largely impenetrable, at least since the separation of the Western Church from the Eastern. From the moment when Sir William Jones of the British East India Company made up his mind to learn Sanskrit the epoch began in which actual acquaintance with the immemorial religious and philosophic thought of the East more and more took the place of the thoroughgoing ignorance that had hitherto prevailed. We have seen something of the different nuance with which the threshold between conscious and unconscious, between self and not-self, has always had in that tradition. I believe it would be difficult to exaggerate the importance of this new direct impact of the Eastern mind upon the Western, though I have no time to trace its variously ramifying consequences.

The third event, or development, was the gradual recognition of *imagination* as the most indispensable factor in the production of works of art, and particularly perhaps, of poetry. And here I would emphasize that the essential, the distinguishing feature of imagination, as such, is that the whole concept of it is founded on the assumed intransigence of that threshold between mind and matter of which I have previously spoken. Of course there are images or copies in the phenomenal world of objects also in the phenomenal world, but these are not aesthetically significant. When we think of an image or a symbol, we think of something that is impassably divided from *that of which* it is an image—divided by the fact that the former is phenomenal and the latter nonphenomenal. The mystery resides in the fact that we also assume an all-important relation between the two. Imagination is, in this respect, entirely correlative to post-seventeenth-century scientific method. It depends for its existence on the exclusion of any so-called "supernatural" operation. Perhaps this is brought out most clearly when we contrast it with its predecessor in the terminology of aesthetics: *inspiration*. For inspiration implies, in a greater or less degree, the actual possession of the poet by a nonphenomenal being other than himself. I am not of course referring to the watered-down tradition, in persuance of which an eighteenth-century poet would still invoke his "muse," but to the deadly serious doctrine of *mania* (divine frenzy, divine possession, *enthousiasmos*)—of which the drawing-room "muse" was no more than a faint echo —the doctrine that prevailed, as E. R. Curtius puts it in his book *European Literature and the Latin Middle Ages*, "through the entire millennium which extends from the conquest of Rome by the Goths to the conquest of Constantinople by the Turks." [5] *Mania* amounted of course to the advent of an actual visitant from the farther side of the threshold to the hither side. If we want to understand the concept, the idea of inspiration, we must think, not of the eighteenth- or nineteenth-century poet decorously invoking his muse in the seclusion of his study, but of something more like what happened to the Cumaean Sibyl before she began to speak to Virgil. And perhaps the best way of observing the gradual process by which the concept of inspiration disappeared and that of imagination entered to take its place, is to study in some detail the histories of some of the technical terms that comprise the uncertain vocabulary of aesthetic discourse; to trace, for example, the progress of such a word as *genius* from its original meaning of "a tutelary spirit," parallel but by no means identical, with the human personality it accompanied, down to its modern meaning.

And what is its modern meaning? This is a thing about which there is perhaps no very general agreement. But all, or nearly all, seem to be agreed on this: that it is proper nowadays to think of genius as something that functions "within" the man rather than in any sense outside of, or separable from, him. Yet there is still a noticeable reluctance to identify the genius wholly with the personality, and indeed there are great difficulties in doing so. It is almost as though the problem for the theorist of imagination is to retain the concept of inspiration, while at the same time rejecting it! Thus Coleridge spoke, in connection with Shakespeare's genius, of his "possessing the spirit" instead of being "possessed by it," and elsewhere he refined his notion to "the genius within the man of genius." "There is," he writes in his *Essay on Poesy or Art*, "in genius itself an unconscious activity; nay, that is the genius in the man of genius." [6]

Today I suppose we tend to identify, or at least to connect, a man's genius with his unconscious being rather than with his self-conscious personality, and we are very ready to locate that unconscious as "within" rather than "without" him, though what we mean by "in" and "out" in such a context is never very clear. The point I wish to make is that, whatever we mean, there is still, by the very nature of the unconscious, that forbidding threshold between the two dimensions of his being. When a man speaks or acts as genius, his unconscious is operative at least *as well as* his self-conscious personality, if not sometimes actually instead of it. You will note that I have said "his" unconscious, though it could well be argued that I was not justified in doing so. Whether that other, that unconscious side of the threshold, is indeed to be included under the heading of "self" and, if so, whether wholly or only partially, would appear to be just the sort of question around which those who are interested in image and metaphor and symbol and meaning (myself among them) are apt to buzz like flies around a honeypot, or wasps around an intruder.

Now very different considerations apply to the exercise of imagination, on the one hand, and, on the other, to any attempt to *investigate* its nature. The poet remains content with the fact of the threshold, whether it is regarded as fixed between self and not-self, or between conscious and unconscious, or between mind and matter; indeed he works with it, avails himself of it. It is the force of gravity to the overcoming of which his athletic power of jumping is directed, but *without* which he could not exercise that power at all. It is different with the theorist. *He* is obliged, however much he may dislike the idea, to apply his ratiocination not only to this side of the threshold, but also to the other. For, in investigating the working of imagination in symbol and image, he is almost by definition investigating the relation between the two sides; and it is simply a fact that you cannot consider the *relation* between two things or states unless you know something about *both* of the two things themselves.

The existence of this very great difficulty renders all the more surprising a cultural phenomenon that I seem to myself have been noticing for some time now: namely, that the general level—I would even say the general level of achievement —of philosophical criticism (that is of talk *about* such things as poetry, images and metaphors, and much that is related thereto) has for some time been considerably higher than the general level of the poetry itself that is being written in our time. But since that kind of talk is precisely the kind we are all engaged in, and lest it should be thought that I am inculcating an unbearable complacency, I hasten to ask the question I have all along been leading up to: namely, can we nevertheless feel that the directions that kind of talk has been taking, and the features of the problem on which it has been concentrating, are really the most fruitful ones? "The talks continue," as we so often read in political bulletins when some high-level conference is in progress. Can we really feel that the talks are in a very satisfactory state?

I do not personally feel that we can. And it is here I believe that Krishna's warning to Arjuna and Blake's aphorism may both be relevant considerations for us. The *Bhagavad-Gita*, you remember, emphasizes that the two sides of the threshold must be kept distinct from one another. Blake insisted that "single vision" is disastrous. And here let me interpose that imagination and a faculty of "double vision" seem indeed to be almost inseparable. When Blake supposed someone asking him if, looking at the sun, he did not see "a round thing somewhat like a guinea," he replied: "Oh no, no, no, but an immeasurable Company of the Heavenly Host crying Holy, Holy, Holy is the Lord God Almighty." He did not in my view mean by this that he was incapable of *also* seeing something like a guinea. Had that been so, he would have been mad. Imagination, in fact, presupposes "double" vision and not simply the substitution of one kind of single vision for another. It requires a sober ability to have the thing both ways at once. May it not be that, if we have reached a stage at which both sides of the threshold are now to be found "within" us, instead of one side being within and the other without—if what was once inspiration is now imagination—nevertheless we must not lose sight of the fact that there is still that threshold between them.

If we do lose sight of it, as I suggest we have been tending to do, if for instance we endeavor to speak, or even to think, of the further side in ideas formed only on this side, in categories of thought and modes of speech, which are almost by definition only applicable to this side, then an unhappy consequence seems to follow. I venture to nickname this unhappy consequence "the curse of Babel" because the Tower of Babel may be seen as the symbol of an endeavor to penetrate a threshold—the threshold between earth and heaven—by using materials exclusively manufactured on the hither side of it. And I am thinking of the danger (when some of those concrete inklings from beyond the threshold are seized hold of and converted into abstract propositions) of our getting more and more involved in a kind of spider's web of increasingly abstract, increasingly contentless, and increasingly sesquipedalian jargon, of which the final effect is only to fatigue and bewilder ourselves and our readers—and perhaps to provide an array of new and legitimate targets for the prowling hosts of linguistic analysis.

If, on the other hand, we fall into the opposite error—if we remain vividly aware of the threshold—but at the same time overlook the fact that it is now within ourselves—then there appears to ensue an unhappy consequence of a different kind. This is perhaps the curse of Zacharias (who, you will recall, was stricken dumb on coming out of the Temple—that is, on recrossing the threshold). Here the threshold, in spite of its being within us and thus under the ultimate jurisdiction of our own wills, is still treated as though it were the old Kantian one between the knowable and the forever unknowable. According to this attitude, though we may have inklings of eternity and moments of ecstasy to which we can refer, we cannot *speak* of, we cannot *express* the nature of, the further side at all. All we can really do therefore is to place that very impotence on record. Personally I believe this view embodies a deep and all-important truth and I believe that it is well that this truth should be expressed, well moreover that it should be expressed both discursively and poetically and by different people, and more than once. But further than that I cannot go, and I cannot, in particular, see any future for it. Because, whatever melodious cadences or cunningly emphasized absurdities the message may be wrapped up in, I believe there is a limit to the number of times a man can profitably inform his neighbor, or be informed by him, that the inexpressible cannot be expressed.

You see the dilemma in which I suggest we tend to find ourselves. Either we strive to discuss metaphor, symbol, image, and meaning in the ordinary terms of logical discourse—in which case, because imagination almost by definition transcends logic, we become entangled in a more and more complicated mesh of thinner and thinner intellectual abstractions; *or* we cut through that Gordian snarl by proclaiming that meaning is something that cannot be talked about at all. But if that is indeed so, and if it also applies to the robes of meaning, her images and her symbols, then the outlook for further books of this nature is presumably poor!

It is true that, as an alternative to falling silent altogether, I have sometimes heard it said that the meaning of a poetic symbol can indeed be spoken of, but only in other poetic symbols. This would mean one point of view on the subject still being confronted with another, but not by way of dialectical exchange—only by way of contrast or competition. If *this* is the correct view, it would seem that future discussions about metaphor, symbol, image, and meaning will be much less like symposia and much more like what the Welsh call an eisteddfod, or like what used to happen from time to time at Nuremberg in the time of Hans Sachs—a competition between rival Meaning-singers.

Personally, I only see one way out of this difficulty. Since it is not an easy or an obvious way, my attempt to adumbrate it is, I fear, going to involve me in all sorts of sins of omission and commission, in reckless assertions, rash prophecies, provocative heterodoxies. To begin with an example of the last—and thus to get it over and done with—I have been coming to feel for some time that imagination, *as an end in itself*, is a vein that has been, or very soon will be, worked out. I am in doubt whether much more that is really significant can be done with it.

Professor Kathleen Coburn, in her introduction to the edition of Coleridge's *Notebooks*[7] that she has in hand, commits herself to the statement that "interest in the theory of imagination has now become almost synonymous with interest in Coleridge." In the belief that she may be right, I have thought fit to put what I now have left to say in the form of an exposition and interpretation of some of the principles and conclusions arrived at by Coleridge in that long period of his life that elapsed after he himself had passed from the exercise of imagination in poetry to the business of thinking and talking about imagination in general.

In the first place we must be clear that poetic imagination was only one aspect of the imagination in which Coleridge was interested. I am not here referring to his distinction between "primary" and "secondary" imagination, but to that concept of what he calls the "philosophic imagination," to which is devoted practically the whole of the long preparatory chapter that immediately precedes the chapter of his *Biographia Literaria* in which that other famous distinction is made.

In the second place Coleridge was acutely aware of that "threshold" of which I have been speaking here and aware of it in its most highly sharpened Western form, that is to say, he was aware of it as being fixed at once between self and not-self, between mind and matter, and between conscious and unconscious. That was why the words "subject" and "object" occurred so frequently in his vocabulary. "Subject" to him meant the self as active mind. "Nature" was "all that is merely objective." "Matter" he defined as "that *of which* we are conscious but which is in itself unconscious." [8]

Thirdly, he was interested in imagination as the best-known means of preserving a right relation between the two sides of the threshold. And it was precisely because the threshold is also a threshold between conscious and unconscious that imagination could perform this function. It could do so because, as he puts it, there is a "consciousness which lies beneath or (as it were) behind the spontaneous consciousness natural to all men" or, as he also puts it, because the mind "can be rendered intuitive of the spiritual in man (i.e., of that which lies on the other side of our natural consciousness)." [9]

What did this becoming "intuitive of the spiritual in man"

signify? Some moment of ecstasy, some inexpressible, unrepeatable high spot of generally enhanced awareness, such as LSD without meaning, as well as poetic symbolism without meaning, can probably supply? By no means. It was a form of *knowledge*, but of a knowledge that is to be won only *with the help* of imagination. And this involved the whole being of the knower, not, as in logical discourse, of his brain only. It is well enough known that Coleridge held that poetry involves "bringing the whole soul of man into activity." It is much less well known that he held the same view about what he called "the knowledge and acknowledgment of ideas."

What then does he mean by ideas? He has told us in many different ways in many different places. In what follows I shall have to content myself largely with a series of quotations.

Mere impressions and notions are not "ideas"; why? "Because they lack the activating power of the will." "Ideas correspond to substantial being, to objects the actual subsistence of which is implied in their idea, though only by the idea revealable. To adopt the language of the great philosophical Apostle, they are spiritual realities that can only be spiritually discovered." And again: "There is a gradation of ideas, as of ranks in a well-regulated army." [10]

What it is that Coleridge meant by the word "idea" can only be grasped when we have also grasped his distinction between understanding and reason. The understanding is the isolated intellect of each one of us, but the reason that irradiates it is superindividual. It was because Coleridge was psychologist as well as philosopher, and it was because the superindividual reason is also the unconscious (of which we normally become conscious only as "matter"), that he could develop his concept of the philosophic imagination as the organ by which that irradiation is accomplished. Again, it is because the threshold between unconscious and conscious is now also the threshold between matter and mind that he could see in the ideas of reason the true link between the hither and the farther side of the threshold. For the idea is neither subjective nor objective. What in its subjective aspect is idea, in the objective aspect may, for instance, be a law of nature.

To identify, as he did, the unconscious self with super-individual reason involves the transference of "the unconscious" from the category of the unknowable to the category of the specifically knowable. Thus, he affirms in the *Biographia Literaria* that, just as "all the organs of sense are framed for a corresponding world of sense," so "all the organs of spirit are formed for a correspondent world of spirit, though the latter organs are not developed in all alike." [11] When the two sides of the threshold are neither prudently distinguished in the mind nor truly united in the will, the result is either the confusion of Babel or the *O Altitudo*! of an impotent silence. When the two opposite sides of it are run together in the understanding, with the insulating membrane between them rudely torn and shattered, they explode in the resulting short circuit into a chaotic pus of the meaningless or the absurd. It is otherwise when the two are held separate, yet united, in the tension which is polarity. And this is what happens when the idea, which is neither objective nor subjective, is intuited or realized by the philosophic imagination. Then it is that the threshold becomes like Aladdin's ring, yielding new meanings for old and giving birth to a future that has originated in present creativity instead of being a helpless copy of the outwardly observed forms of the past.

There remains the question of terminology. It may be argued that this so-called philosophic imagination, supposing it is admitted, is something so different from poetic imagination that the same label ought not be applied to both. I think that is very likely so. It may well be that a *generalized* awareness of the further side of the threshold is the ultimate goal, the *ne plus ultra*, of anything that can, with due observance of linguistic usage, be signified by the term "imagination."

A particularized awareness, an advance from excited inkling to sober knowledge, could be another matter. The task of imagination, as Coleridge himself has defined it, is to apprehend the "unity in multeity" of the objective world. When his further researches led him on to approach the further task of apprehending the multeity in unity of the subjective world, it may be that he would have done better to draw his distinction, not between poetic imagination and philosophic imagination, but between imagination in general and something else. I want in conclusion to suggest that the proper name for this something else would have been "inspiration"—but an inspiration very different from the old type of inspiration—the *mania*, or "possession," which was the historical predecessor of imagination. I would suggest that the inspiration that Coleridge dimly divined as the *successor* of imagination is to be a transformed inspiration, an interiorized one. Yet I would give it the name of inspiration, because it involves the notion of some communication with individual entities, individual beings beyond the threshold; and this was also characteristic, though in a different way, of inspiration in its former sense.

Such a faculty, such a development of epistemological method, will of course reach out far beyond the realm of literature and of talk about literature. It would, for example, be as indispensable to my M.I.T. professor and his associates as to the creative writer. The planners of the future shape of society need it no less urgently. That does not trouble me, for I feel that literature, like many other things, is most itself when it is reaching out beyond itself. *Within* the realm of literature, and particularly of the use of imagery and metaphor, I seem to see it leading to many changes. Indeed, the final prophecy I shall hazard is perhaps my greatest heterodoxy of all. For I am inclined to see any advance from imagination to inspiration as entailing the sort of change that sounds at first more like a retreat than an advance—like a retreat to some of the types of semantic usage we generally regard as superseded.

Thus, one of the outstanding characteristics of all kinds of "tensile" language, as opposed to "steno-language" (if I may adopt Professor Wheelwright's useful terminology)[12] is that it has many meanings, or potential meanings. The vehicle of a metaphor, for instance, may be fixed enough, but the tenor is polysemous—and thus ambiguous also. I think we may now have to find terms and phrases of which the *tenor* will be monosemous—though it will still be the tenor of a vehicle, and not a piece of steno-language. That was also a characteristic of the mode of personification, and of allegory as opposed to myth or symbol. Personification is monosemous and it is not ambiguous, yet as long as it continues to be uttered and apprehended with "double vision," it functions as a metaphor—even (as Professor Morton Bloomfield pointed out in February, 1963, in an article in *Modern Philology*) as a metaphor with especially vigorous potentialities. I do not see us profitably returning to the rhetorical devices of personification and allegory as they were known in the past, but I do hazard the prophecy that, if imagination advances towards transformed inspiration, it will be accompanied by something like a transition from metaphor to transformed personification and from myth and symbol to transformed allegory. It will be a question of finding a kind of tensile language that is not merely polysemously suggestive, but of which the words convey reasonably identifiable and repeatable meanings— the kind of meanings that we can hold, so to speak, between our lips and taste and explore them with our tongues while we do so, though if we attempted to seize them with our teeth they would collapse into dust.

One of the things that images, metaphors, and symbols do is to develop and strengthen our faculty of imagination. For without that we soon find that we can make nothing of them. It could be that, in a time still to come, this faculty, once it has been so developed, will be valued, not primarily as an end in itself, but rather as a preliminary training in a whole new way of using language—a way that will be neither vague and inaccurate on the one hand nor rigid and definition-ridden on the other. Language so used would be the true utterance of "double vision" inasmuch as it would embody a simultaneous, and yet not an *intermeddling*, awareness and acceptance of both the two opposite sides of the threshold. And it could be that it is only in some such language that effective and badly needed inspirations from beyond the threshold that is fixed between the subjective potency of humanity and its objective perceptions can ever be either uttered or apprehended.

NOTES

1. *The Bhagavad-Gita*, II. 18.
2. *Ibid.*, XI. 9.

3. The letter to Thomas Butts is dated November 22, 1802, and is cited in William Blake, *Letters*, ed. Geoffrey Keynes (New York: Macmillan 1956), p. 79.

4. Cf. I. A. Richards, *Principles of Literary Criticism* (New York: Harcourt, Brace, 1928); and *Coleridge on Imagination* (New York: Harcourt, Brace, 1935).

5. Trans. Willard R. Trask (New York: Pantheon, 1953), p. 474.

6. Samuel Taylor Coleridge, "Essay on Poesy or Art," in *Biographia Literaria*, ed. (with his aesthetical essays) J. Shawcross (London: Oxford University Press, 1962), 258.

7. S. T. Coleridge, *Notebooks*, ed. Kathleen Coburn (New York: Pantheon, 1957).

8. S. T. Coleridge, *Biographia Literaria*, I, 174-75.

9. *Ibid.*

10. Cf. *ibid.*, II, 259.

11. Cf. *ibid.*, I, 167.

12. Cf. Philip Wheelwright, *The Burning Fountain: A Study in the Language of Symbolism* (Bloomington: University of Indiana Press, 1954), and *Metaphor and Reality* (Bloomington: University of Indiana Press, 1962).

III

LITERARY
RESOURCES IN
THE INTERPRETATION
OF MEANING

> *... dichterisch wohnet*
> *Der Mensch auf dieser Erde.*
> —J. C. FRIEDRICH HÖLDERLIN

✳ THE PREVIOUS sections on religion and philosophy have explored the possibility of nonobjectifying interpretation. The first focused on the relation between the language of theology and religious meaning; the second, on the relation between the interpretations of philosophy and the poetic act. The essays in those sections are agreed in implying that an understanding of the poetic imagination is important to the specific rhetorical tasks of theology and philosophy. The question raised here is: What *are* the literary resources contributing to the interpretation of meaning? This is to ask the value of the poetic model for nonobjectifying discourse.

Hölderlin's saying speaks indirectly to this issue. Man lives for meaning, and the poetic act (*poiēsis*) is a paradigm for the creation of meaning. Thus the man who "dwells poetically on the earth" lives meaningfully.

Kenneth Burke interprets this to mean that "man is a symbol-making animal (*animal symbolicum*)." He distinguishes man's symbols as "semantic" and "poetic":

The first would try to *cut away*, to *abstract*, all emotional factors that complicate the objective clarity of meaning. The second would try to derive its vision from the maximum *heaping up* of all these emotional factors, playing them off against

79

one another, inviting them to reinforce and contradict one another, and seeking to make this active participation itself a major ingredient of the vision. This poetic meaning would contain much more than pragmatic, positivistic, futuristic values . . . So, the poetic vocabulary, when complete, will take us into-and-out-of (the complete play with its exhilaration at the close) . . . While the semantic vocabulary would, I think, unintentionally cheat us, by keeping us without, providing a kind of quietus in advance, never even giving the dramatic opposition a chance, avoiding the error which Lucretius made, at the sacrifice of his work as "science" and to its gain as "poetry." (*The Philosophy of Literary Form*, 1941)

Burke continues this interpretation here in "A Theory of Terminology." Using drama as a model, he contrasts the realm of motion (as in the behavioristic, *semantic* meaning of scientific interpretations) with the realm of action (as in the aesthetic, *poetic* meaning of literary interpretations). In this way he devises a theory of the meaning-functions of words based on the literary resource of drama.

Beda Allemann moves in a direction different from Burke. Instead of opposing poetic and scientific interpretation, he presents poetic language as a third mode of expression between rational discourse and emotive expression. Allemann writes in *Über das Dichterische* (1957): "We little understand and little know how to express the realm of poetic language which lies between rational and emotive expression (*den zwischen Bereich*). Poetic language surpasses the other two by participating in both."

In "Metaphor and Antimetaphor," Allemann adds to the knowledge of the poetic "between-realm." Using Kafka as the primary example, he describes a particular poetic act in which the resulting text is a metaphor without an external reference for comparison. Such an "antimetaphor" or "absolute metaphor" refers only to itself and thereby makes possible meaning which is *neither* in opposition to *nor* dependent upon logical, semantic definition. It is totally free from any prerequisite "rational order of the universe that can be represented adequately by a network of rational analogies." In antimetaphorical literature the "meanings of words are activated . . . so that a meaningful context is constituted."

Both critics use literary resources to inquire into the way meaning comes into being. Burke provides a theory of the symbolic and nonsymbolic functions of words based on a dramatic perspective. Allemann formulates the concept of "antimetaphor" and shows that it allows creation of meaning in a world where traditional references for meaning are lost. Thus, these literary resources, whether brought to bear on the methodology of theological, philosophical, or literary interpretation, operate in the creation of a nonobjectifying language, in understanding the power of human imagination, in "dwelling poetically on the earth."

5
Kenneth Burke:
A Theory
of Terminology

I

I SHALL START with a most difficult matter, a report of five dogs.

First, there is the "primal" dog, the dog that one usually encounters in a "primal scene" of childhood. He has a strong, unmistakably Freudian strain in his make-up. And he is crossed with what Malinowski would call "context of situation." That is, he merges into the background (benign or malign) of which he was an integral part when the child originally learned to distinguish him. Though both he and his context may have been forgotten in their particulars, the *quality* of the experiences associated with him may stay with us throughout our lives, figuring subtly ("subliminally" would be the word now) in our attitude towards dogs. And under the influence of drugs, hypnosis, or psychoanalytic couch-work many particular details about him and his context of situation may be recovered. The main point for our purposes is that he is not properly defined in terms of his own peculiar nature alone. He is "symbolic" in the sense that an essential part of his "meaning" (both forgotten and unerringly remembered from out the recesses of our past) resides in his role among a complex of conditions *not* specifically doglike.

Next, there is the "jingle" dog. Whereas the "primal" dog would be associated with many nonverbal circumstances, the "jingle" dog would involve his relation to the particulars of speech (such as the fact that in English the word "dog" rhymes with words that the corresponding *Hund* or *chien* would not rhyme with; and by a tonal accident that engaged the poet, Cummings, he is "God" spelled backwards). Here also would belong his *proper name*, plus the punlike relationship to identical or similar names, including those of people or places. One might even extend the range of the "jingle" dog to cover the logically dissociated linguistic situation that unites dog and tree (since each, in its way, has an association with the word "bark").

But though the "primal" dog and the "jingle" dog can tug dangerously at the leash of reason, all is quite different with the "lexical" dog, the kind defined in the dictionary *per genus et differentiam.* Viewed by the tests of either poetry or neurosis, he is an exceptionally uninteresting dog. But without him and his kind, the world of wholesome common sense as we know it would collapse into gibberish. In our civilization, to indicate what the word "means," you wouldn't even need a verbal definition, or the corresponding word in some other language. A mere picture of the "lexical" dog would suffice to indicate what was meant, even in a language that we did not know. Yet note, for later reference in this chapter: It's impossible to make a picture just of "dog," in the specifically *lexical* sense. For there are all sorts of dogs, dogs of many sizes, breeds, shapes, colors, postures, and so on. But your picture would require you to draw some *particular kind* of dog, while at the same time your illustration must be interpreted as indicating what is meant by the word "dog" *in general.* And as a matter of fact, the picture in an alien dictionary might have been not of "dog" in general, but of a *fox terrier.* Also, within this narrower orbit, the same sort of problem would prevail. For even the picture of a fox terrier requires you to use specific traits for general purposes, since all fox terriers differ from one another. Here's a problem to which we must certainly revert, as regards questions that have to do with a Theory of Terms.

Fourth, adapting from Aristotle, we'd distinguish an "entelechial" dog, the "compleat" dog toward which all doggery variously aspires, to the extent that dogs fulfill their nature as dogs. We here confront the terministic principle involved in an expression such as "perfect" dog, to designate the natural fulfill-ment of dog *qua* dog. Obviously it's much easier for a dog to be wholly a dog (to exemplify the very dogginess of dog) than it is for a human being to exemplify in all fullness the humanity of his nature as a human being. I hope later to make clear how this formalistic principle figures in our thoughts on the functions of terms. But for the present, we must merely introduce the notion.

Finally, there is the "tautological" dog. You get him by crossing the "primal" dog with the "lexical" dog, though this experiment works only if you continue to select among the off-spring, not all of which breed true. He should reveal the "pri-mal" strain only in the sense that, like the primal dog, he merges with his context. But he does so in a way typically "lexical." For instance, it would be a "tautological" step if we went from "dog" to "kennel," or to "dog food," or to "dog license," or to "master," or to "cats," "hunt," "game," subservience, loyalty, running in packs, doggedness, etc. When approached thus, from "dog" as point of departure, all such related details become "tautological" in the sense that they are all infused with the "spirit" of the term in terms of which they are mutually related (somewhat as though "dog" were at the center of a circle, and all the other terms were distributed along the circumference, as radii generated from this center).

In some early pages entitled "Examination of a Case De-scribed by Rivers," [1] I first ran into a simpler form of the dis-tinction I am trying to make here. It involved a speculation of this sort: A child who had been frightened by a dog in a passage-way from which that child could not escape might be traumat-ically affected by the *situation of being confined in a passage-way without an exit at a time when a danger sign was present*, thus responding to this whole Gestalt as fearsome motive, rather than more specifically to the dog in particular as danger sign. And if the child's attention had been formed along those lines, the resultant "affect" in an adult might show up rather as *claustrophobia* (fear of *closed places*) than as *fear of dogs*. The *situational* aspect of the case could manifest itself particularly (as with the war phobias that Rivers was treating) when the sufferer had to enter a dugout under circumstances marked by the nearness of the enemy. For he "unreasoningly" *feared* the only part of the situation that might bring him some comfort: namely, the opportunity to "dig in" and thus to be less of a target for the enemy's bullets.

But note that, as regards either the "tautological" dog, or the "primal" dog, their definition involves their *contextual* or *situational* nature, their meaning as part of a *scene*. This is the important consideration for our next step. But before we move on, let's briefly review our list:

1. *Primal dog.* Associated with submerged memories of a "first" dog, in case the experience was in some way formative, or "traumatic." Inseparable from his context of situation.

2. *Jingle dog.* Involves sheerly tonal associations, most of which are accidental to one particular tribal idiom.

3. *Lexical dog.* The wholesome, common-sense, dictionary meaning—and if the world had only that, we'd all die of boredom, or perhaps fare forth imperialistically to interest ourselves by making other people suffer for our fear of boredom.

4. *Entelechial dog.* Becomes of major importance in works of art. For instance: ideally, a character who is to be sacrificed must be the perfect victim for the given situation. The person who is to exact the sacrifice must be, in his way, a perfect fit for his role as victimizer, and so on— at least insofar as classical norms of artistic excellence are concerned. And perhaps those who spoke in tongues (we read about them in various passages of the New Testament) were intermingling jingle utterance with entelechial meaning. If a situation in adult life were capable of being summed up by some analogy (as with the relationship between an anecdote and its moral in a fable by Aesop) the representation would be "entelechial" by reason of its *summarizing* nature. However, it might be translated into terms of a merely *imaginary* incident *falsely* "remembered" from one's infantile past. The entelechial principle is a purely formal,

nontemporal kind of fulfillment. But it can be represented in narrative terms, i.e., terms for *temporal* priority. One can confront a situation now by entelechially imagining the kind of "primal scene" that would "account for" things as they now seem to be. In this sense, the imagined scene would be entelechial, a condensed, formal way of *fulfilling in principle* what is to be "unfolded." Freud's concept of a "repetition-compulsion" would also fit in here. For such a motive contains "entelechial" ingredients insofar as the sufferer, or subject, almost as though by deliberate design, "perfects" different situations by imposing upon them the same essential relationships.[2]

5. *Tautological dog.* Such associations as one might build up by inert answers to a questionnaire. You'd ask people what they thought of when you said "dog," and you'd weed out the meanings that seemed idiosyncratic. For your main interest would involve the most representative associations of ideas. Even brilliant stylistic innovators build their figures of speech by not venturing far from such standard channels of affinity, though often (as I tried to show in *Permanence and Change* when discussing "perspective by incongruity") underlying properties of correlation may be contrived by perspectival leaps, as in Friedrich Nietzsche's style, with its modes of abrupt reclassification, basically a method he could have learned from Spengler or Ezra Pound, had he had the opportunity.[3]

II

I discovered the need for these several dogs when trying to settle on a hard-and-fast distinction between signs and symbols. The distinction is clear enough at its extremes. For instance, smoke is a sign of fire, and fire may be the sign of a short circuit. But smoke may be the symbol of a communication between "upper" and "nether" realms. And fire may be the symbol of sexual agitation, or of cleansing (as in purgatory), or of hellish punishment. (Or, for that matter, it may be the symbol of all such implications, indeterminately interwoven.

Surely much of the lure in images derives from the ease with which they can contain motives that, if reduced to equivalent terms logically explicit, are found to be violently at odds with one another.)

But not only is there a vexing area of overlap between symbol and sign. The distinction does not seem useful enough to me even at its best, except in extreme cases, as when we assume that, although bees apparently have a quite complicated and exact signaling system, the present state of the evidence would not allow us to class them with man, as capable of "symbolic action" in the full sense of that term. They are presumably *born with* a signal system, whereas man must *learn* his symbol systems. And we must put bees into a different classification from man at least until some investigator can prove by his experiments and observations that bees' ways of signaling to one another are not innate, but the bees must go to school and take courses in Bee! Apparently birds perfect their songs by imitation, but sing somewhat even without training. And in any case, I submit that "symbolic action" in the full reflexive sense prevails only with man, an animal that can apply conventional symbol systems to the discussion of conventional symbol systems.

But before proceeding further, I must amend my references to the "tautological" dog. The tautological relationship among terms is most profitably studied if we work with specimens at a much higher level of generalization than such a concrete word as "dog." There are at least two grand instances: (*1*) The Cycle of Terms Implicit in the Idea of "Action"; (*2*) The Cycle of Terms Implicit in the Idea of "Order." I tracked down the "Action" set in my *Grammar of Motives*,[4] though without wholly knowing what I was doing. The "Order" set I worked out with methodological awareness, in my *Rhetoric of Religion*.[5] I submit that these two terministic dynasties have reigned conjointly through much of our civilization, maybe through *all* civilizations (or "cultures," if you want to add Spengler's distinction between "civilization" and "culture").

You might well choose to build a third cycle around "Power." I once made a beginning when, in connection with

Richard Wright's novel, *Native Son*, I tentatively offered this line-up for the Power family:

> It is composed of many members: social power, sexual, physical, political, military, commercial, monetary, mental, moral, stylistic (powers of grace, grandeur, vituperation, precision)—powers of emancipation, liberalization, separation ("loosing"), powers of fascination and fascization ("binding," as in Mann's "Mario and the Magician")—and powers of wisdom, understanding, knowledge. There are ways whereby, owing to the nature of synechdoche, any member of this family may come to do vicarious service for any other member, or for the family as a whole—so that one may marry or rape by politics, wage war in argument, be mentally superior by the insignia of social privilege, bind or loose by knowledge, show one's muscle or enhance one's stature by financial income, etc., in whatever permutations and combinations one cares to contrive. In particular, in *Native Son*, I should have liked to discuss the author's treatment of the interrelationships among the powers: physical, sexual, social, and monetary—with at the end a transcendence into the powers of understanding.[6]

Freud's nomenclature suggests a related strand, a Cycle of Terms Implicit in the Idea of "Unconscious Repression." In fact, every book can be studied as a family of terms thus implicating one another in some analogous fashion. Here, for instance, is a relevant passage concerning a book by John Dewey, *Liberalism and Social Action*, built about the persuasive force of terministic interrelationships:

> About the topic of liberalism, the author groups the cultural values he most admires. His book is written to show with what important and desirable traits liberalism can be identified. He goes through a cycle of virtues, such as peace, liberation, "the development of the inherent capacities of individuals made possible through liberty," tolerance, reintegration, science, rationality, education, charity, courage, and hope—and he pleads that liberalism, as he conceives it, can be included in this cycle.

And I analyzed Hitler's *Mein Kampf* as a vicious use of this same principle, there contrived by pitting a conglomerate batch of "Aryan" virtues against a correspondingly indiscriminate

batch of self-contradictory vices that might be found in vary-
ing degrees everywhere, but that Hitler attributed exclusively
to his chosen Jewish scapegoat. (Both of these examples are
reprinted in my *Philosophy of Literary Form*.)[7]

We have already considered a kind of terministic generation
closely linked with the "entelechial" principle. For a further development here, consider the relationships among the cast of
characters in a drama. Thus, if a certain kind of effect is to be
produced, then a certain group of persons must be chosen for
their function in bringing about that effect, and their relationships to one another must be so designed that all the *dramatis
personae* can make their particular contributions to the necessary development of the plot, in the necessary order. Here, too,
is a kind of terministic cycle, with the characters functioning
as key terms, their nature as simulated personalities residing
somewhere between the grand generalized cycles and the realm
of our concrete "dog," but also involving appropriate imagery
as an auxiliary resource to the ends of individuation and actuali-
zation.

I should feel uneasy if I had to keep these various kinds of
terministic cycles trimly related to one another, so that I might
make a composite photograph of the lot. Rather, I would turn
that whole subject around, and call attention to the fact that
much of the *freedom* in man's capacity for symbolic action resides precisely in the range of improvising here open to him,
even when working with a public idiom, a medium of expression
collectively shared by all the members of his tribe. A cycle of
terms is like a cluster of stars. The sky, as viewed from any one
of such positions, will show a corresponding difference in the
distribution of the other positions, though they all ultimately
form but one single set of interrelationships. And it is in this
way that a man defies total prediction until he is finished. Indeed, prediction is in effect the application to living man of
parameters derived from the realm of death; that is, the possibilities of the future are reduced to terms derived from the past.

But implicit in a range of terms, each of which can provide a different perspective, there is by the same token the possibility of improvisation, involving a quite different distribu-

tion of terms. And this is true every time until the last time. A new incident, for instance, can prod us to see "good" implications in a term that heretofore we had used pejoratively; whereupon a corresponding revision of related terms might ensue; and here are the makings of a "conversion." In sum, the very range and shiftiness of the terministic cycles we have been considering contains ingredients that link the powers of symbolic action with the possibilities of innovation. Hence, in the hopes that I have established this point at least well enough to free me from the need for a single overall pattern here, let me refer to still another way of cutting up the realm of terms.

It has to do with some thoughts I once had on Whitehead's statement that "philosophy is the product of wonder." At the time when I first ran across this good formula, I was also much exercised by Veblen's term, "idle curiosity," to designate the ultimate motive behind philosophic and scientific speculation. On asking "How do these terms relate to each other?" I saw, or at least thought I saw, the possibility of a graded series here. Toning things down step by step from "wonder," I figured that we might get successively: interest, curiosity, "idle curiosity," and play. That is, philosophy might be called "the product" of any such motive, on that scale of graduated attenuations. Or, proceeding in the other direction, one might go *gradatim et paulatim* from wonder to reverence, thence to awe, and so on to fear, dread, terror—whereat, striking out at an angle, we might call philosophy a mode of defense, or of cowardice, or of courage. (This graded series was discussed in my *Permanence and Change*.)

For the moment, I would like to point out that, to some degree, terms are thus modified continually. Usually what happens is that, as Bentham schematized in his "Table of the Springs of Action," the same motive can be presented in either friendly or unfriendly guise (his words are "eulogistic" and "dyslogistic"). Thus frequently, on a smaller scale, you may find an author recommending under a favorable label much the same principle or process he had dismissed elsewhere under an unfavorable one.

So much for a general statement about the resources of persuasive terministic exercising. Though you might gladly settle for less "freedom," in the hopes of making things better stay put, I submit that such liquidity is intrinsic to the nature of symbolic action. In any case now, with our five dogs and our variously constituted cycles of terms at least waveringly in mind, let's worry through a third major aspect of terminology.

III

To approach this problem, note first that the Power family of terms comes to a fearful focus in the realm of *motion*. That is, in the last analysis, you cannot be "powerful" unless you *move* something. An orator might prove himself powerful by goading his audience to battle. But the ultimate test is still stricter: namely, can those who were thus goaded to battle ultimately succeed in so throwing their weight around (by their sheer powers of motion, as enhanced by the motions of their fighting machines) that they *physically* undo the enemy?

In this sense, I'd say that our concern with the Power family centers in problems to do with the relation between "action" and "motion." Many terministic schemes that prevail today are essentially concerned with the modalities of motion. This proposition applies to all the physical sciences. The *scientists themselves*, in working out their terminologies, are decidedly in the realm of symbolic *action*. But the *terminologies* are primarily concerned with the realm of *motion*. Similarly, if one designs a thermonuclear bomb, or devices in the realm of chemical or biological warfare, he is *acting*. But the *devices* that he designs exert their power purely in the realm of *motion* (except, of course, insofar as their mere existence may serve to strike terror in the enemy, and thus can also be a kind of sheer imagery that "acts" as a deterrent to an opponent's policies).

So, I dare think that in our way we are fully recognizing the very *essence* of the Power family when we build a theory of symbolic action around the frank recognition of the conditions imposed upon us by the requirements of sheer motion. Indeed, one cannot even so much as think a thought (or internally say a word!) except insofar as there are certain neural motions in his brain primarily, and perhaps secondarily throughout all his body.

But though there cannot be any "act" of "thought" (or whatever you want to call it, "verbalization," for instance) without corresponding bodily motions, symbolic action is not reducible to terms of motion. In brief, the man who designs and programs a computer is *acting;* his computer is nothing but a set of *motions*—and one cannot legitimately reduce the designer to terms of his design. To give the most obvious instance of the error involved in the attempt to define human action in terms of a computer's motions, bear it in mind that, at the very least, man is a biological organism, whereas a computer is an *artifact.* And how can a device that does not undergo the motives of pleasure and pain possibly serve as an adequate model for the motives of any animal, even one much "lower" in the scale than man? I put "lower" in quotation marks, because many of man's typical vices, such as one people's bullying of another people, do not make me unduly proud of our specifically human prowess.

But basically, it all gets down to this: Destroy all animals that are endowed with our characteristic kind of "symbolicity" —and there would still remain such motions as the rotation of the earth on its axis, the revolutions of the earth about the sun, and the periodic surging of the oceans in response to the influence of the moon primarily, and of the sun somewhat. In brief, there would still be the irreducible realm of sheer motion. But if we take, as part of the given, man and his special powers of "symbolicity," we confront a formula of this sort: *Persons act;* in the process of *acting,* they must *move; things* can but *move.*

But here a problem enters. It concerns, of all things, the relation between the literal and the analogical. We seem somehow to have got so turned around that, if you treat man as a sheer machine, you are thought to be literal whereas, if you draw a distinction between a machine's motions and the machine maker's actions, you are more likely to be called figurative because you don't call a man a machine (if not a machine old-style, then the new type, of which the electronic computer is the model). So we must ask: Just what *is* "literal," and what "analogical"?

In one sense, the nature of language is such that *every* use of a word is "analogical." For if I apply the same word to two situations, I can't escape being involved at least in a kind of "proto-analogy." For every situation, in its clutter of details, is unique. Hence, if I apply the *same* term to *two* situations, I am necessarily stressing an element they have in common, as distinct from their differences (and in his *Rhetoric* Aristotle makes it quite clear that analogy is involved when a speaker defines a current situation by treating it in terms of some past situation).

Surely, when we talk about *situations*, this ambiguity is obvious. We know that no two historical situations are exactly alike. But how about our words for *things?* Let's approach the matter by a slightly new start.

A friend who teaches drama had written me celebrating the "dramatic metaphor." He was referring to the grand terminology that centers in words for active, passive, and reflexive, terms that also tie in with the distinguished "Stance" family, connecting "essence" and "sub-stance." Nor should we overlook their analogues in current terminologies of motion: effectors, or output; receptors, or input; and feedback (terms that I would have us look upon as *fragments* of a Dramatistic perspective).

But, whereas some years ago, I would have settled on the notion that we here had to do simply with a metaphor, I most decidedly do so no longer. Things *do but move*, and persons *do act*, though persons can also let themselves get pushed into the role of mere automata, little better than things in motion, as when they respond unthinkingly to the goads of a spellbinder, and fall to thinking it is their patriotic duty merely to do as they are told.

Drama would figure here only secondarily, in the sense that, by using drama as a model, we can get good cues as to what range of terms is implicit in the idea of an act (a range that even includes, as with tragedy, the concept of cure by vicarious victimage).

My friend answered: "All language is metaphorical." And since there is a sense in which he is correct, let's see what we should do next. First, we can note that even if all language is metaphorical, or analogical, there is obviously a difference between calling the moon "moon" and calling it, say, "wandering daughter of the night." So, at the very least, there are metaphors and metaphors—and one of these expressions is clearly much more figurative than the other.

Yet, on closer inspection, even our literal term dissolves into etymologic origins that take us far from a literal one-to-one correspondence between a "thing" and its "name." Thus "moon" merges into "month" ("mooneth," as we get "warmth" from "warmeth," if we may follow Horne Tooke in these matters), and both apparently dissolve into a root *me* or *ma*, meaning to "measure," from which there also is derived our word "meditate."

Hence, to size up this terministic situation adequately, we are required to recall the instance of the "primal" dog, which could not have existed alone, but was necessarily part of a "primal scene." We are here involved in the line of thought, essentially Spinozistic, that reminds us: No "sub-stance" can exist all by itself, except "everything." If the object that we literally designate as the moon were all by itself, no poet would ever have written a poem about it, and no spaceman could ever hope to reach it; or, for that matter, we could not even know of its existence.

The particular items of our experience can exist at all only because each is part of a wider context. We are usually misled here by the nature of the "lexical" dog, a drawing of which can be shown without a background (except, of course, the page itself, which is rightly ignored as part of the definition).

To grasp the essential nature of language, we must not think of speech as essentially a process of "naming" things or situations. Rather, since every thing or every situation is in some respects unique, insofar as we apply the same word to more than one thing or one situation, we are in a sense "analogizing." (Hence my reference to a kind of "proto-analogy," as distinct from analogy in the explicit, formal sense.)

If one cries "help" in three totally different situations (say, when in danger of drowning, in danger of falling, in danger of being struck), he has in effect "classified" all three different sets of circumstances under the same general heading, as "help-situations." Or, otherwise put: He has in effect given all three situations the same "title," because of some important element they have in common, despite their great differences as regards particulars. And I submit that we should think similarly of outright "names" or "nouns" ("substantives"). Our words for individual "things" do not involve a mere one-to-one correspondence between symbol and symbolized (word and thing). Rather, they are a kind of *abbreviation* (Horne Tooke's suggestive term) that can serve to entitle a situation by featuring whatever part of that situation happens at the time to be of primary interest.

Thus, every time I encounter a dog in real life, the dog is in a somewhat different situation. But all of these situations could be entitled "dog-situations" insofar as that aspect of all the many different actual or possible situations is what particularly engages the center of my attention. All of these situations doubtless have more things than the dog in common. For instance, all of them will necessarily be situations that have in common the same laws of nature. But we don't think of these when referring to a dog-situation under the title of "dog," though we immediately become conscious of such a situational ingredient if we are making plans for sending a dog up in a satellite.

If you adopt this contextual or situational approach even to terms for specific acts or concrete objects, you see that they are, in effect, titles for complex situations, much as the word *Hamlet* sums up, in terms of the name for the most significant role, the vast complexity of details subsumed under that title. The title, though applied literally to one particular drama, is "proto-analogical" in the sense that it can be applied to performances differing greatly from one another. And it becomes *outright* analogy when we apply it to some person, real or imaginary, whose situation in life might lead us to call him "a Hamlet." [8]

All told, although in my earlier book, *Permanence and Change*, I primarily stressed the metaphorical or figurative aspects of language, and treated philosophical "perspective" as a kind of "analogical extension," I would now want to shift the emphasis, contending that, first of all, we have to do not just with metaphors, but with *terms*, and *relationships* among terms. On this basis, it is *literal* to say that "persons *act*, and things but *move*." And it is *figurative* to say that people are like their own machines, or that their computers can be taken as an adequate model of their motivational structure.

True, man is prone to the temptations of automatism, and he cannot act without moving—but to say as much is not by any means the same as saying that he is "nothing but" a bundle of sheer motions. Observations concerning the rules of a game are *not* identical with the sheer distribution of forces that one would necessarily perceive if he were not able to infer that the event under observation was a game being played purposively by persons, and if he could analyze the game not in terms of players trying to score in accordance with a rule book, but only as things in motion, with a near-infinity of relationships involved in their sheerly physical behavior and in the measuring of stress and position with regard to one another. Imagine trying to figure out what is going on in a ballgame, if you were being strictly "extrasymbolic," hence could not even know what is meant by strikes, and balls, and hits, and runs, and errors, and innings, but could work your way to the rule book only by correlating various weights in motion on a field. Then, if you were caught in all that nightmare entanglement of terms for sheer motion and position, imagine what a lifting-up it would be, if of a sudden you were allowed to read the rules of the game (which is to say, if you were told what *principles of action* inform the game), and could *deduce* the game's near-infinity of motions *in terms of* this principled realm as motivational source rather than *reducing* the game solely to terms of such motions.

I don't know why I picked on *moon* for my example. And surely I could have got a better *metaphor* than "wandering daughter of the night," though there is our spacemen's ambition to make a "soft landing" on (shall we say?) "Cynthia." In any case, I hope I have made it clear that, be they literal or metaphorical, we are in the realm of *terms*. Even the sheer sensations of the body report to us *in terms of* sight, sound, smell, and so on. And thus, too, to match "proto-analogy," there is a kind of sheerly physiological "pre-nomenclature" (in the realm of sheer motion) which reduces all sorts of particular situations to terms of one or another sensory channel.

IV

Along with thoughts on the range of terms, including the special *energeia* of metaphor and image, we might comment on the particular nature of the printed page, and its similarity to a musical score. Either might happen to be handsome. But regardless of how either might *look* when judged sheerly as calligraphy, as visual design, its *major* function resides in its nature as instructions for performance. When we see a *musical score*, regardless of whether or not we are musicians, we realize at a glance that it is a set of instructions. We do not ask that it itself have music's peculiar sensory quality as appeal to the *ear*. For we assume without question that this test is not met until the work is performed by an expert. But because we have all learned how to talk and to read, we don't usually stop to consider the implications of that fact that, in a notable respect, print on a page is exactly like musical notation. That is to say, the reader is like a performer, who may or may not be able to carry out the printed instructions adequately.

True, there is a sense in which even a painting or a piece of sculpture must be "performed" by the observer. It cannot come to life for him unless he "empathizes" with it. In this sense, a painting or sculpture, in its nature as a symbolic act, cannot be any "better" than the observer's ability symbolically to "re-enact" it. Hence, in this respect, examples of graphic and plastic art are also but "instructions for performance." Yet they differ from the printed page or the musical score to the extent that they are already *finished performances* done by experts, whereas the printed page or the musical score are not "final performances" in that sense. The music is yet to be *played* (either *for* us or *by* us, or in the imagination of those comparatively few persons who are skilled enough at reading a score to judge the sounds internally without the need to hear them, as with Beethoven who was deaf). And we do not usually stop to remind ourselves that the instructions on a printed page are not a performance (in the way that a painting is a performance) until the text is read, either to us by an expert reader, or to ourselves as performers more or less capable of imagining how it sounds, even if read in silence.

See where we are then, in trying to understand the nature of symbolic action. *All works* involving symbol systems depend for their effect upon our willingness and ability to *collaborate* by responding properly to them. Within these conditions, we can distinguish between the kinds of works that are already a final *performance* (such as drawings, paintings, sculpture, singing, recitation, the playing of musical instruments, dancing, acting) and texts that are *instructions* for a final performance (such as musical notation and words on a page). One should keep this distinction in mind when speculating on the "sensory" nature of different media.

Yet, a further distinction is necessary here. All music must be appreciated in terms of its sensory nature (that is, we must first of all love the rhythmically related sounds as such before we can ever "transcend" this *sensory* experience and hear unheard melodies, by advancing from the realm of sensory appreciation to an intuition of the *principles* involved in such an experience). But in contrast with musical notation, there are many kinds of *verbal* utterance that have no value whatever, as regards the tests of tonality and rhythm.

Understandably, amateurs or analysts concerned with the wonders of poetry or prose as *spoken* (as glimpsed through and beyond the *written* words) are scandalized at the very thought of "speed-reading." For insofar as a text is adapted to the pace of the voice, an approach to it by speed-reading is at best vulgar.

Yet much information that comes to us through words has no specifically verbal value. Someone might wisecrack with the contents of a phone book, and bring out funny resonances. But usually even that same enterpriser, who might find there material for an entertaining *tour de force*, ordinarily consults that batch of names simply as a convenient way of getting a number.

And, in contrast with the norms of poetic or rhetorical pacing, the ideal here would be an invention that fed into you, as into an indifferent computer, that whole condensed mass of information without a single concern for anything other than its ready availability.

Insofar as education involves, among other things, the acquiring of much purely factual data, we would be best off if we could take in such material, not just at the sluggish pace of speed-reading, but rather with a computer's lightninglike capacity to "scan" and "remember" the vast clutter of information that flashes before it. And the situation would be best of all if, like a computer, we didn't have to exert ourselves consciously in such a process of storage, but could have the data somehow communicated to (or stuffed into) our brains electronically, while we played or slept or concerned ourselves with other matters.

We might well keep such thoughts in mind, when comparing the symbolic action of written or printed words with the symbolic action of other artistic media, including the poetry or rhetoric of the spoken word. Otherwise, we might ask the wrong thing of the written or printed word, which cannot be wholly "tactile" until spoken.

True, there can be direct visual appeal, as with calligraphy or fine printing—but in this sense the appeal is not specifically verbal at all, since it is purely the appeal of *design*. I would by no means underrate the value of such appeal. I merely want to bring out the fact that the sheerly *verbal nature* of words is not concerned with visual design except insofar as the design of a poem on the page can also help indicate how the text should be *recited* (or should be *heard* in the imagination). As compared with the pace of the voice, the eye tends always to be *somewhat* of a "speed-reader." And placement on the page may serve, though inadequately, as a poet's equivalent of a musician's instructions for performance (such as *largo, moderato, adagio,* and the like, or as a musicologist's indicating of the basic beat in terms of metronome, with signs for acceleration or retarding, and for changes in volume).

But we should keep in mind that the page itself is not the

performance in the sense that a painting is a performance. It is like a scantily edited musical score, which leaves much to the judgment of the reader *as* "performer."

V

We have said nothing yet of the relation between dialectical "transcendence" and dramatic "catharsis" (between the Upward Way and victimage). Nor have we considered a possible third logological step (from self-expression and communication to "consummation," the sheer "tracking down of terministic possibilities" because one sees them, or thinks one does, implicit in a given terminology, and one cannot rest until such potentialities are actualized). However, you "get the idea." And surely, of especial moment among "tautological" correlations there is the "thinking of the body," the translation of motivational attitudes into terms of corporeal analogues. Another name for these might be the "metonymic principle."

But by way of concluding, let us dwell on a simpler thought, of this sort:

In the world as we know it, there are many kinds of conferences, consultations, symposia, and the like, dealing with words and meanings. Usually, somewhere in the course of them, participants fall to bewailing the inadequacies of speech. Yet, but for speech, any such enterprises would be almost impossible, even as regards meetings of experts in other forms of symbolic action.

For a parting sunshine thought, let us look at the matter thus:

Think how happy each one of us is, whenever he chances to say something, even if it be but a single sentence, that someone else agrees with. And if we are outright praised for our offering, we swell with pride (though usually hastening to adopt a measure of what Marianne Moore has astutely called "judicious modesty").

Just think, then: What if, far beyond the presenting of our tiny inventions, we had invented the *realm of words itself*. How we would love ourselves!

The thought might help remind us how greatly we do prize that miraculous medium, The Word. And if I may quote from a former dear friend of mine, whom I also necessarily broke with (for how could one but break with someone to whom one had been so close?):

> There is peace in the sequence of changes fittingly ordered: vegetation is at peace in marching with the season; and there is peace in slowly adding to the structure of our understanding. With each life the rising of a new certitude, the physical blossoming free of hesitancy, the unanswerable dogmatism of growth. Who would not call all men to him—though he felt compelled to dismiss them when they came, communion residing solely in the summons.[9]

NOTES

1. Cf. Kenneth Burke, *Permanence and Change: An Anatomy of Purpose* (New York: New Republic, Inc., 1935), pp. 136-42.

2. Cf. Sigmund Freud, *Beyond the Pleasure Principle*, authorized trans. from the second German edition by C. J. M. Hubback (London: The International Psychoanalytical Press, 1922).

3. Cf. Burke, *op. cit.*, p. 90.

4. New York: Prentice-Hall, 1945, pp. 227-74.

5. Boston: Beacon Press, 1961, pp. 183*ff.*

6. Kenneth Burke, *The Philosophy of Literary Form* (rev. ed. abridged by the author; New York: Vintage Books, 1957), p. x.

7. *Ibid.*, pp. 309, 164-89.

8. For a fuller development of this position see my article, "What Are the Signs of What? A Theory of 'Entitlement,'" *Anthropological Linguistics*, IV (June, 1962), 1-23.

9. The lines are from a novel of mine, *Towards a Better Life* (Berkeley: University of California Press), that was published over thirty years ago, and that was reissued in 1966.

6

Beda Allemann:
Metaphor
and Antimetaphor

TECHNICALLY, METAPHOR MAY BE easily defined. In fact, the definitions of metaphor we find in Aristotle and Quintilian have never been superseded; they may even be applied literally and still serve as the basis for modern attempts to redefine the concept of metaphor. According to Quintilian, a metaphor is a shortened simile. "Achilles fights like a lion": this is an explicit and complete simile.[1] What Achilles does is compared with what a lion does, and the act of comparing is gramatically expressed by the word "like." But if I say, "On the battlefield Achilles is a lion," this is a shortened simile, a simile lacking the grammatical indicator for the act of comparing. If one would interpret this sentence in a purely naïve way, as a translation machine, for instance, might interpret it, one would read it as a statement that Achilles was in fact a lion. But an intelligent reader or listener will realize at once that, in spite of the lack of the *term* indicating the simile, this sentence does not state a downright identification of Achilles and lion but rather is a simile. Achilles is not meant to be a real lion, but he is merely compared with a lion, though in an abbreviated or telescoped manner of expression, that is, without an explicit grammatical indicator. The common element on which the comparison is

based, the *tertium comparationis*, is easily recognized: Achilles
and the lion are equally characterized by valor and strength, so
that on the basis of these qualities Achilles and the lion may
very well be compared. If reader and author agree on this basis
of comparison the expression may be abbreviated even more.
In this case it would be possible to speak only of the "lion on
the battlefield," and everyone would know that Achilles is
meant. In other words, "lion" is used here in a figurative sense
(*im übertragenen Sinne*); it is a paraphrase, a way of expressing
something in an indirect way. The presence of an analogy that
can be traced by logical thinking is essential for understanding
a given metaphor as well as the phenomenon of metaphor as
such.

So far everything seems clear and obvious to such a degree
that I should apologize for mentioning things everyone knows.
But it is necessary to recall the traditional basis of our concept
of metaphor before we can deal with the complex problems we
have to tackle when we now begin to look more closely into
this matter and especially when we ask what metaphors in modern literature are like and in what ways they are used.

I might add here that literary critics often do not use the
term metaphor in the strict sense of classical rhetoric. In such
cases metaphor tends to take on the meaning of "image." However, the term "image" is again a metaphor.[2] This is why I
would like not to deal with it here and instead concentrate on
an attempt to find out what a metaphor is.

It cannot be denied that metaphor in poetry is supposed to
increase the graphic or sensuous element (*Anschaulichkeit*) of
language. Our example of Achilles and the lion may show what
I mean by this. The name Achilles by itself has certainly no
particular *Anschaulichkeit*. The metaphor "lion" for "Achilles,"
however, does possess this quality that poetry traditionally
is supposed to have. This might lead us to believe that here we
have found the basic motive for the use of metaphor. It would
seem that using metaphors makes sense as long as it contributes
to the increase of *Anschaulichkeit* in the text. Thus it makes
sense to call Achilles a lion, but for the same reason it would
make no sense at all to call a lion the Achilles of the animals.

At first glance this line of argument seems convincing. However, we recall that in certain phases of literary history just such artificial and abstract (*unanschaulich*) metaphors were highly popular. These phases were the phases of Mannerism in literature. Now many critics believe there is a particularly close relationship between the technique of metaphor as used by Mannerist poets and certain ways in which modern poets handle their verbal material. If we take this relationship into account and if we think of the important role of the obscure and impenetrable metaphor in modern poetry, it seems indeed a rash conclusion to locate the essence of metaphor in its *Anschaulichkeit*. It may very well be that it has been the *Anschaulichkeit* of the conventional metaphor that has caused many modern poets to regard metaphor with reserve and even distrust.

Let us look more closely at the roots of this problem. I think at this point we will find most helpful what Nietzsche said about metaphor in his short essay "On Truth and Lie in an Extra-Moral Sense" (*"Über Wahrheit und Lüge im aussermoralischen Sinn"*),[3] written in 1873. This essay is the most explicit record of what Nietzsche thought of metaphor; to be sure, metaphor is treated here no longer in a purely technical or rhetorical context, but is the object of metaphysical reflection. Nietzsche discusses metaphor here as the basic characteristic of language and of poetry in particular. The idea of metaphor being the origin of language may be found before Nietzsche, in Giovanni Battista Vico and Herder. But with Nietzsche this insight into the metaphorical quality of language generates a crisis that, I think, is most significant for the attitude of modern literature toward metaphor. Nietzsche interprets the Greek term μεταφορά literally, as *translatio*, "carrying over." But unlike the ancient teachers of rhetoric he does not regard this *translatio* as being restricted to the technique of replacing one word by another or one group of words by another; that is, he not only thinks of the technique of *immutatio verborum*. Nietzsche discovers the metaphorical *translatio* taking place even before language itself comes into being.

His basic question is in what way the data of sensual perception may be articulated, that is, in what way they may be translated into language. The first metaphor the human mind uses in the act of cognition is the translation of sensual perception into an image. Only through another metaphor can this image be translated into language. For Nietzsche both these metaphors are "leaps out of the original sphere into a radically different and new one." The concept of metaphor is taken here in a fundamental epistemological sense. The *translatio*, the leap, takes place even before the first word is articulated. The drive to create metaphors is the "fundamental drive of man." [4] Language is made of metaphors and nothing else, while the *Ding an sich* that the metaphors denote cannot be discerned. Nietzsche notes that men are hardly ever aware that they use nothing but metaphors when they speak. The explanation for this is that the original metaphors have worn out in the course of time. Scientific terms belong to the last stage of this development; it merely *seems* that they express their object exactly and completely, while in fact even scientific terms are "residua of metaphors." [5] Thus even the language of science is revealed as being basically metaphorical. Nietzsche speaks at this point of illusion, deception, make-believe, distortion and dream.

Nietzsche believes that the language of poetry has one great advantage over the language of science. Unlike science, poetry deliberately reactivates the metaphorical quality of language. In poetry the widely used and worn-out metaphor, which is no more recognizable as such, is replaced by original metaphors intense with *Anschaulichkeit*. Poetry uses metaphor in a free, playful, and ironic manner. In poetry metaphor wins back its original color, spontaneity, and freedom. Poetry is a deliberate deception—but precisely through this deception poetry corresponds to the basically illusionary character of language. Thus poetry finds itself in a peculiarly ambiguous relation to reality. This ambiguity is emphasized in the title of Nietzsche's essay, in the opposites "truth" and "lie." In *Thus Spake Zarathustra* we read, "The poets lie too much." [6] It is obvious that Nietzsche does not mean here a subjective moral failure of the poets. They do not lie because they lack love of truth. On the contrary, the metaphorical character of language forces them to lie. By lying deliberately, that is, by using an explicitly metaphorical language, they are closer to truth than those who lie without being aware of it. In a way, the poets are liars in the service of truth. Poetry is paradoxically involved in the dialectic opposition of truth and lie. Since the time poets have become fully aware of it, this precarious position has become manifest frequently and in various forms in modern literature. Its direct consequence is the situations of crisis peculiar to the consciousness of the greatest modern poets. An analysis of what these poets felt about metaphor and how they used it thus can illuminate their historical situation to a surprising degree.

We have now established the basis necessary for taking a closer look at metaphor in modern literature. We started with a brief refresher course on the purely technical and rhetorical meaning of the term metaphor as it has been determined in classical antiquity. We proceeded to consult Nietzsche about the possibility of a metaphysical interpretation of the metaphorical quality of language. In accordance with Nietzsche's predominant way of thinking in his first period, "metaphysical" in this context is synonymous with "epistemological." In order not to be misunderstood, I should add here that by quoting Nietzsche I did not imply that today we still might agree in all points with his analysis. From the point of view of the history of philosophy, Nietzsche's epistemology and the radical scepticism deriving from it are now outdated. Most of all the phenomenological school of thought has convinced us that such scepticism is in its way no less naïve than that naïve realism against which Nietzsche fought. As seen from the position of phenomenology, Nietzsche's epistemology and even that of the neo-Kantians must seem a fruitless blind alley. It cannot be denied, however, that precisely in aesthetics and literary theory Nietzsche has exerted a tremendous influence and has been responsible to a high degree for the ways modern poets have understood their role as poets. Certainly this applies first of all to the German-speaking countries, where the close relation between the ideas of the most eminent poets and Nietzsche can be clearly demonstrated and often has been emphasized by these poets themselves. But in a wider sense I think it applies also to modern literature in general. If we do not insist on a too-narrow concept of direct influence we might very well say that all modern literatures have been affected by Nietzsche's diagnosis of a crisis of the European mind, by his insight into the nature of nihilism, and by his attempt to overcome this nihilism by specifically artistic means.

On the other hand, there exists in twentieth-century literature a close parallel also to the phenomenological triumph over the epistemology of scepticism. In literature the ironic and hermetic elements of *fin de siècle* and symbolist art gave way to an emphasis on a new immediateness (*Unmittelbarkeit*) in poetic language. In Germany this change was particularly radical; with it a new period in literary history began that today is known as Expressionism. In this context it is highly significant that it was in Expressionist circles where for the first time the battle cry against metaphor arose. Carl Sternheim, one of the most successful dramatists of Expressionism, was the first to articulate the condemnation of metaphor and to make it his artistic program.[7] Another dramatist of the same generation joined the battle and in 1917 published a "Programmatic Essay Against Metaphor" (*Programmschrift gegen die Metapher*); this author was an Austrian by the name of Theodor Tagger, better known under his pseudonym Ferdinand Bruckner.[8] Gottfried Benn, who in his early period was one of the greatest Expressionist poets, spoke not very many years ago in a summary of his views on poetry ("Probleme der Lyrik," 1951) of his distrust of the ἐπίθετον ὤρνανς and the simile introduced by the word "like."[9] I think he was right when he called this distrust the basic artistic tendency of his generation. The language of poetry was thus to be made more powerful and intensive and a new immediateness (*Unmittelbarkeit*) was to be achieved in poetry by avoiding metaphor. This tendency may be regarded as a parallel to the tendency of phenomenology to "return to the object" (*zurück zu den Sachen*). In literature this tendency is by no means peculiar to German Expressionism alone. A similar attack on metaphor may already be found in Marinetti's *Manifesto tecnico della letteratura futurista* (1912).[10] The distrust of metaphor survives long after the periods of Futurism and Expressionism. Only a few years ago Alain Robbe-Grillet, one of the leading authors of the French *nouveau roman*, mounted an attack against metaphor that was no less radical than the Expressionist manifestoes.[11] At first glance, Expressionism and Futurism seem to have nothing at all in common with *nouveau roman*. On the one hand there was the grandiloquence of the leaders of a revolution in style; on the other hand, the ascetic soberness of a new realism. But these two radically different literary schools had one tendency in common: the rejection of metaphor.[12]

Now, doesn't this seem to refute Nietzsche's idea of the metaphorical nature of language and poetry? Whatever arguments may be brought forward, the rejection of metaphor implies the belief that within the medium of language there is a possibility of a more immediate access to reality than by way of metaphor, which, after all, is merely something like a paraphrase. From this point of view the new theories against metaphor indeed contradict Nietzsche's theory of art. The twentieth-century authors I have mentioned are convinced that metaphor cannot but hide the true nature of things from our eyes instead of revealing it as it is, which is the task of poetry. By making the indirect, figurative (*uneigentliche*) expression appear in place of the direct or proper (*eigentliche*) one, metaphor is a downright lie. But it is surprising that seen under a different aspect this argument completely agrees with Nietzsche's views. Nietzsche had deliberately accepted metaphor as illusion and lie. In his poetry metaphors abound, and this, by the way, is the main reason why his prose poem *Thus Spake Zarathustra* today seems rather dated and smacks too much of the less attractive aspects of the nineteenth century.

But is it enough just to wage a battle against metaphor in order to get a language of poetry free from metaphors? I think it is hardly surprising that shortly after publication of *Manifesto technico della letteratura futurista*, Alfred Döblin, the German Expressionist, criticized Marinetti for having never overcome in his poetry the metaphorical language he had outlawed in the *Manifesto*.[13] If it is true that language is originally metaphorical, that even scientific terms can only be the product of a metaphorical act, of a *translatio*, then it must be impossible to

avoid metaphor in poetry, in spite of all manifestoes and proc-
lamations against metaphor. From this point of view the rejection of metaphor is merely a special aspect of the ambiguous
position of the language of poetry between truth and lie as
dialectical opposites, as Nietzsche has described it. And now it
is no longer necessary to ask whether metaphor in poetry is
admissible or not. Instead we have to ask the more complex and
indeed more interesting question: how modern poets can come
to grips with the metaphorical nature of language in spite of
their openly declared dislike of metaphor and in spite of their
being aware of the fact that metaphors and images in the manner
of Nietzsche's *Zarathustra* are impossible today. There is no
simple and general answer to this complex question. Only when
looking at the *oeuvre* and the language of one particular poet at
a time can this question become a fruitful one. I choose Franz
Kafka for such a closer look because I believe that his case will
give us particularly deep insights into the problems we are discussing here.

In Kafka's diary we find a sentence that is highly significant
in this context: "Metaphor is one thing among the many that
make me despair of writing." [14] Now Kafka takes for granted
here that it won't do to write without metaphors. At the same
time this insight that metaphors cannot be avoided causes despair. Here we have one of those moments I mentioned earlier
in which the problem of metaphor opens our eyes to a fundamental crisis, a crisis in which modern poets again and again are
faced with the question whether poetry is still possible at all.
Elsewhere in his diary Kafka turns against the abstract metaphors he finds in Dickens, an author he had for some time regarded as his ideal.[15] By abstract metaphors Kafka understands
metaphors that have no inner necessity but arbitrarily introduce
an utterly disparate *tertium comparationis* into the sentence.
Certainly Kafka does not mean here some stylistic blunder in
Dickens. We rather have to take it that for Kafka—and Kafka's
contemporaries—every metaphor must have been out of the
way, ill-fitting, and "abstract" in this particular sense. Kafka illustrates his point with a passage from one of his early prose
pieces:

> The poplar in the fields swaying in the wind, which you have called the Tower of Babel—for you refused to believe that it is a poplar—now is again without a name and you will have to call it "Noah when he was drunk." [16]

The abstract, arbitrary metaphor gives no satisfaction and immediately has to be replaced by another one, and so *ad infinitum*. Kafka adds:

> Look what you are doing! Out of sheer rashness you are not satisfied with the true names of things, they are not enough for you, and now, in a great hurry, you pour arbitrary names out over them. Quick, quick! But as soon as you have run away from them you have forgotten their names. [17]

Kafka calls this a "seasickness on land." But what may be done against such a seasickness? Certainly you can restrict your use of metaphor as far as possible, as Kafka did in his mature prose. You can go even further and return to the practice of explicitly indicating with grammatical means that your metaphors are mere similes. The late Kafka went even so far as to use a simile and then to mention this fact explicitly, for example with the words ". . . but this is only an image." This critical attitude towards his own manner of expression and the habit of first using a simile and then partially retracting it are both highly characteristic traits of Kafka's style. [18] They correspond exactly to that structural characteristic of Kafka's works which may be described as a continuous modifying and retracting of what at first seemed an absolutely positive statement and what at last turns out to have been a mere hypothesis. Kafka applies this basically simple technique with great subtlety, and it effectively prevents readers of a Kafka novel or story from arriving at a convincing interpretation of the whole story though the details are narrated with great realism.

This technique, however, is not yet Kafka's final answer to the metaphorical nature of language and to the necessity of using metaphors in poetry. Indeed it is obvious that he tried to reduce metaphor, to relativize the metaphors he used, but such a purely negative technique alone would hardly produce great poetry. Kafka really aimed at something else, which is the secret of the extraordinary success of his prose texts; this is perhaps most clearly revealed by the short prose piece "Prometheus," written in 1918. This text runs as follows:

> There are four myths about Prometheus. According to the first myth Prometheus was bound and his fetters were forged to the Caucasus, because he had betrayed the Gods to men, and the Gods sent eagles which ate from his ever-growing liver.
>
> According to the second myth Prometheus, the beaks hacking at him, pressed himself in his pains against the rock, deeper and deeper, until he became one with the rock.
>
> According to the third myth his betrayal was forgotten in the course of the millenniums, the Gods forgot, the eagles forgot, he himself forgot.
>
> According to the fourth myth they became tired of what had become pointless. The Gods became tired of it, the eagles as well, and the tired wound closed.
>
> The inexplicable mountains remained.—The myth attempts to explain what cannot be explained. Since its ground is one of truth it has to end up in what cannot be explained.[19]

From among the four versions in which Kafka presents the myth of Prometheus, the first and the last ones are especially important in our context. The first version is a concise account of the complete myth of Prometheus fettered to the Caucasus. According to the last myth only the mountains remain and they cannot be explained. Kafka ascribes this striking reduction to the fact that all who take part get tired and forget. This reduction may be read as representative for a certain process in literary history. When we recall Kafka's novel *The Trial*, and especially *The Castle*, we will remember that the beginning of the decisive phase of an event is indicated by the key figures forgetting and getting tired. To be sure, new insights in the usual sense of the word are impossible at this stage, because everything has been forgotten that formerly might have been used as material for a mythological interpretation. At this stage also the strength is lacking that would be necessary to draw practical conclusions from a possible new insight. Nevertheless this last stage in which everything has been reduced to what cannot be explained may be taken as the point at which Kafka aimed in his stories and novels. For a long time the myth of Prometheus has belonged to the traditional repertoire of European literature. The complete myth of the first stage may be interpreted freely and serve as the basis of fruitful variations, as for instance Goethe's Prometheus hymn and many other works based on the same myth, written before and after Goethe. In all these works Prometheus represents a titanic and suffering superman or over-man. The name of Prometheus may be used in similes and parables. Kafka deliberately cuts off all these possible references. As early as after the second of Kafka's four versions, Prometheus becomes identical with the rock to which he is fettered. He loses his character as a unique mythical figure that may be quoted. At the end, only the pure fact of the inexplicable rock remains. It would be going too far to say that the fourth version is plainly the ideal pattern of Kafka's own narrative technique. Indeed his works are as impenetrable and inexplicable as that rock, but it is obvious that such a rock taken by itself can no longer be the object of literature. The inexplicable mountains of the fourth version derive their meaning from the preceding three versions. The basic structure in all of Kafka's stories seems to be precisely this: the circumstances and possible explanations of what happens are reduced step by step to a core that can no longer be explained. In view of what I have said before, a way of writing like this might very well be called antimetaphorical. In the first and most complete version of the myth of Prometheus a most comprehensive *tertium comparationis* is given: in this version Prometheus may be interpreted as the representative of all mankind. In the last stage of the reduction there is no comparison whatever possible. It would be as senseless and arbitrary to compare the mountain with anything else as to compare a poplar with Noah being drunk or with the Tower of Babel.

It has become common practice in Kafka criticism to call his tales parables. Critics agree, however, that such parables are not the moralizing fables of the eighteenth century.[20] Kafka's parables are no exemplary stories that may be deciphered by extracting a moral from them. Kafka's prose texts avoid metaphor and thus become a kind of metaphor themselves; this new metaphor, however, is without a definite level of meaning outside of it, a level on which its "real," nonfigurative, *eigentliche* meaning may be found. This paradox may be confusing at first glance, but if you look more closely you will see its inner logic. In texts like Kafka's all similes are deliberately suppressed; everything that is said is severed step by step from any conventional associations. The result is a peculiarity. I would like to put it this way: a text like that becomes the metaphor of itself. Metaphors are based upon relations the reader has to know beforehand, either through his own experience or through the literary conventions familiar to him. This is also true for the unusual, far-fetched metaphor or "conceit." A text like Kafka's prose parables, however, which has torn down the bridges of metaphor, necessarily becomes a metaphor whose only frame of reference is itself. By avoiding metaphors that may be isolated as single stylistic figures here and there in the text, the parable as a whole is a kind of absolute metaphor.

I hasten to admit that I am using here a somewhat precarious terminology. In the first place, I call the whole of a text a metaphor, which means that the term "metaphor" loses its technical, rhetorical meaning with reference to a clearly defined single element of style. But we have no other choice when a text obviously does away with the single metaphors contained in it, as Kafka's texts do. Secondly, and this is more important, it is a downright *contradictio in adjecto* to talk of an "absolute metaphor." A metaphor always has its origin in a simile, and therefore it can never be absolute. Nevertheless modern literature abounds with absolute metaphors, and there are even plenty of single stylistic elements which very well might be called absolute metaphors. This is particularly true for poetry.

I would like to take my examples from poetry now, since in poetry it is easier to isolate examples from the text. I quoted Kafka to show the basic antimetaphorical tendency in modern literature. This tendency finally may cause a whole text to contract into an absolute metaphor. A detailed analysis of an absolute metaphor in this comprehensive sense could only be done at great length and would take too much space here. In lyrical poetry, however, there are smaller units that may be called absolute metaphors. I take as a random example the first two lines of a poem, "Chorus of Things Invisible" (*Chor der unsichtbaren Dinge*), by Nelly Sachs, a poet now living in Stockholm:

> Wailing wall night!
> Carved in you are the psalms of silence.[21]

It is obvious that we will run into difficulties if we try to analyze a passage like this by means of the traditional definition of metaphor. We may even discover here "transpositions" that seem to correspond to the transpositions of the accustomed metaphorical technique. The abstract concept "night" is "transposed" or "carried over" to the concrete and sensuous perception "wailing wall." But we would be at a loss if we were to indicate in a strictly logical way the point of resemblance or *tertium comparationis*. I do not want to say that it is impossible to reconstruct a logical and meaningful relation between "night" and "wailing wall," but at least we would need quite a few words to explain it. When we read the poem, however, the poetic meaning of the succinct passage "wailing wall night" is readily understood, without any lengthy operation of mind being necessary.

The failure of any attempt to find a logical basis of resemblance is even more manifest with the metaphor "psalms of silence." This expression is an obvious paradox, because in the realm of silence there are no psalms. Nevertheless nobody would claim that this poem of Nelly Sachs is nonsense poetry.[22] A "transposition" that cannot be explained logically may have a particularly intense poetic effect. No wonder that literary critics, in order to characterize a phenomenon like this, try to solve their difficulties by using a term that itself is paradoxical, that is, the term "absolute metaphor."

Paul Celan, a contemporary poet, has characterized modern poetry with these words: "In the poem all tropes and metaphors tend to be reduced *ad absurdum*" ("*Und das Gedicht wäre somit der Ort, wo alle Tropen und Metaphern ad absurdum geführt werden wollen*").[23] This is more than just another of the battle cries against metaphor we have heard from the poets for the last fifty years. Celan does not proclaim the death of metaphor; he rather postulates that metaphor should no longer be regarded as being based on a logical comparison. Modern theory illustrates again and again that in practice poets have long since freed themselves from the fetters of the theory of metaphor being an abbreviated simile. Hence it is a purely terminological question whether we should go on using this term in criticism of modern poetry. If we stick to the traditional theory of the abbreviated simile we will have to come to the conclusion that there are hardly any metaphors in modern poetry. Metaphor as a figure of style as defined by traditional rhetoric is indeed dead. But we need not insist on the traditional definition of metaphor. We may recall the basic meaning of the Greek word μεταφορά and concentrate on the act of "transposition," of *translatio* as such; by this understanding a wide new field of inquiry is opened up. The metaphorical nature of language and of the language of poetry in particular will have to be explored anew. What are the laws governing the metaphors that have been reduced *ad absurdum*? And first of all: in what dimension does a *translatio* of this kind take place?

In any case it would be a mistake to believe that the metaphors in modern poetry (or rather what is left of metaphor in modern poetry) simply continue a long-established tradition in Western literature. In Germany this has been done by Ernst Robert Curtius and his school; in particular it has been Gustav René Rocke who in his works on Mannerism disregarded any historical differences in the use of metaphor. On first glance there seems to be a close relationship between the hypertrophic use of metaphor characteristic of Mannerism and the paralogical or absolute metaphor in the modern sense. If we look closer even the boldest and strangest Mannerist metaphor invariably turns out to have retained the firm basis of a rational and conventional analogy pattern. If Mannerist metaphors seem obscure to us, this is only because today we are no longer familiar with the conventions of Mannerist poetry. I quote as an example a line by Jean de Sponde, a French poet of the sixteenth century: "The flesh emits the fragrance of the sweet fruit of present joy." Hocke calls this a paralogical metaphor reminiscent of Baudelaire.[24] Indeed, a thematic similarity with Baudelaire is undeniable, but

I would not call this metaphor paralogical. It is Mannerist in that it contains a bold abbreviation; but the conventional logical pattern upon which it is built is easily recognized. An abstract concept, "present joy," is compared to a "sweet fruit." This comparison does not transcend the Christian conception of sin; the fruit plucked by Eve in the Garden of Eden is supposed to be associated here. And since according to Christian belief the flesh is the sinful part of man, the comparison of the flesh with the fruit is not at all paralogical.

The imagery of the lines I quoted is obviously related to a familiar frame of reference. To deny this would be to misunderstand the nature of Mannerist metaphors. Even great Mannerists like Góngora never go beyond such a rational frame of reference. The only unusual thing about Mannerist poetry is the virtuosity with which these poets established analogies. In principle even the most obscure and abstruse of their metaphors may be deciphered from the context and be reduced to a rational statement. Only one technique of Mannerist poetry may be regarded as a borderline area: the use of the oxymoron. The oxymoron is the most succinct form of paradoxical expression; for instance Góngora speaks of "red snow." Taken by itself, an oxymoron like this is certainly a most alogical phenomenon; indeed its essence consists in a logical contradiction. But when it is used deliberately as a rhetorical trope to achieve a certain effect, it belongs to a rationally constructed system. Even contradiction as such is still a category of logic. Moreover, the meaning of a paradoxical abbreviation like our example may be rationally reconstructed from the context.[25] In spite of its formal similarity it has nothing in common with an absolute metaphor that cannot be reduced to anything.

The same is true for the so-called oppositional metaphor that operates with a negation. We find an example for it in Aristotle's *Poetics*.[26] The shield of Ares is referred to as a "cup without wine." The cup is associated with Dionysus as the shield is associated with Ares. Hence the shield of Ares may be called "the cup of Ares." If this shield is called "cup of Ares" this is the common Aristotelian μεταφορά κατ' ἀναλογίαν. When we go one step further and instead of the "cup of Ares" speak of the "cup without wine" we have an oppositional metaphor. It is true that for an unprepared reader even this example taken from Aristotle seems obscure and hermetic. But for Aristotle it is only a variant of the metaphor of analogy, and for him analogy is something easily expressed mathematically, that is by a proportional equation: the proportion of *a* to *b* equals the proportion of *c* to *d*. We may find such metaphors far-fetched and bold, but in fact they always remain within the limits of a logical construction. The conceit, that is the far-fetched metaphor in the sense of traditional rhetorics, is no irrational phenomenon but rather a triumph of a purely rational talent for combination.

Modern poetry no longer recognizes the essential prerequisite for this art of combination, namely the idea of a rational order of the universe that can be represented adequately by a network of rational analogies. One aspect of this art of combination, however, has been preserved; I mean the technique of abbreviation, of the flexible and rapid confrontation of words and meanings taken from widely disparate spheres. What happens in such confrontations? This is a question that becomes more and more pressing since now it is obvious that the old logical and mathematical concept of analogy is unable to answer it any longer. There is an easy way out if one is content with negative definitions that merely describe the disappearance of the old logical basis of comparison. By speaking only of paralogical, alogical, or irrational metaphors we remain within the limits of the old theory and way of thinking.

Another unsatisfactory answer is to say that metaphors are a product of the emotions or of poetic vision. Such an answer presupposes the basis of poetry to be radically different from and opposed to the basis of rational concepts. But this view, which has been current since the eighteenth century, merely indicates that instead of one extreme the other has been chosen; that is, the rationalism of the old theory of poetry has been replaced by an irrationalism that today seems inadequate also.[27] What we really need is a logic of poetic language that is no longer determined by mathematical logic, but neither does it lapse into irrationalism. In such a logic of language, metaphor could no longer be defined as an abbreviated simile. In fact, metaphor as a clearly defined figure of style in the sense of a rhetorical ornament would no longer play a role. On the other hand, the metaphorical nature of poetic language might become most significant in such a logic. We would have to ask to what degree language is metaphorical even when it contains no metaphors in the sense of figures of style.

I believe that the examples I have quoted from Nelly Sachs may indicate what such a metaphorical language free from metaphors is like. We have seen that expressions like "wailing wall night" or "psalms of silence" cannot be explained fully as metaphors in the strict sense of the traditional systems of rhetoric. Nor would we get any further by interpreting a combination like "wailing wall night" as an identification instead of a simile. A purely linguistic analysis shows that "wailing wall" and "night" do not coincide at all, but are two disparate words standing in juxtaposition. Using the terms of basic school grammar, "wailing wall" may be explained as an apposition to "night." But simply by noting the juxtaposition of the two words, their relation to each other is described only in the most superficial way. The essential question is one that aims at the tension that is always inherent in the juxtaposition of two words in a poem, provided that it is a real poem and not an empty play with words. Grammar and rhetoric deal with the words as they are printed or written, they catalog the words and groups of words according to their kind. Within these limits the two disciplines are of great help; they supply a set of concepts that make it possible for me to communicate with others on certain objective phenomena of language.

A logic of language in the sense I indicated, however, would have to concentrate first on what stands between the lines and between the words, or, to be more precise, what is not patently there, but what appears between them as a kind of magnetic field, as tensions created by the interplay of relations. I think it is justified to speak of a *translatio* or μεταφορά taking place in this "magnetic field" between words. The definition of absolute metaphor is radically different from the traditional definition in that it does not separate the sound and meaning of a word. The traditional definition separated the meaning of a word from its sound in order to transpose this meaning into a different word-sound. "Wailing wall" does not mean "night," and "night" does not mean "wailing wall," but the two words stand in a relationship to each other; they exert a mutual influence, and this kind of *translatio* and correlation opens up a dimension in which an understanding of this verbal structure becomes possible. To understand this particular constellation of words as such requires more than knowing the dictionary definitions of "wailing wall" and "night" to find a point of comparison common to both. To understand it means to penetrate into the specific dimension that is between the words.

At this point I would like to remind the reader once again of Nietzsche's theory. Nietzsche said that language is of a metaphorical nature because it can only speak in an indirect way about things. From this point of view every word is a lie. I have already suggested that this scepticist theory of language must be regarded as outdated. Today we believe that things are present in the words of language. This is especially true for the language of poetry whose quality is determined by the fact that it is capable of evoking reality. If we were to follow Nietzsche and locate the fundamental metaphorical act between the objects on the one hand and the words on the other hand, we would take words merely as signs that necessarily misrepresent reality. Hence reality and truth could never be adequately apprehended. I think, however, that this differentiation between the objects and the words that are supposed to denote the objects is a highly arbitrary act. When language is being put to use it is impossible to separate sound and meaning of a word. On the other hand, a mere accumulation of words, as for example in a dictionary, does not constitute language. It is prerequisite for the possibility of language that words can enter into mutual relations without being separated from their meanings. Here, in what happens between the words, the fundamental *translatio* takes place. Here the meanings of words are activated, put to use and thus become more precise, so that a meaningful context is constituted. To my mind this process seems to contain the essential metaphorical quality of language.

Perhaps I should add that I certainly do not believe that the basic metaphorical quality of language is manifest in modern poetry only and did not exist in earlier periods. One might go as far as to say that for a long time the theory of metaphor contained in the traditional systems of rhetoric has prevented us from perceiving that quality. The traditional theory separated meaning and sound and saw the process of *translatio* under the aspect of a logical and mathematical analogy between meanings. On this basis, metaphor could be regarded as a mere ornament that has only a loose relation to the real (*eigentlich*) meaning of what is said. But by rejecting metaphor or, to be more precise, by reducing metaphor *ad absurdum*, modern literature has made impossible the conventional explanation of the metaphorical nature of language.

NOTES

1. Quintilian, *Institutio Oratoria*, VIII. vi. 8.

2. That was seen already by C. F. P. Stutterheim in his comprehensive work, *Het begrip metaphoor* (Amsterdam, 1941), p. 659.

3. In Friedrich Nietzsche, *Werke in drei Bänden*, ed. Karl Schlechta (München, 1960), III.

4. *Ibid.*, p. 319.

5. *Ibid.*, p. 315.

6. *Ibid.*, II, 383.

7. "Kampf der Metapher" was the motto of Carl Sternheim's *Chronik von des zwanzigsten Jahrhunderts Beginn* as well as the title of the epilogue of his prose text "Ulrike" and of one of his essays (cf. Wolfgang Wendler, *Carl Sternheim: Weltvorstellung und Kunstprinzipien* (Frankfurt/M., 1966), p. 281, note 51). Sternheim explained his distrust of metaphor in more detail in his novel *Europa*. Cf. Carl Sternheim, *Gesamtwerk*, ed. Wilhelm Emrich (Neuwied am Rhein/Berlin, 1963-1964), V: "Prosa II," 276.

8. Theodor Tagger, *Das neue Geschlecht: Programmschrift gegen die Metapher* (Berlin, 1917).

9. Gottfried Benn, "Probleme der Lyrik," *Gesammelte Werke in vier Bänden*, ed. Dieter Wellershoff (Wiesbaden, 1959/1962), I, 504.

10. The Russian Formalists also have, in their theories, fought against metaphor. Cf. Victor Erlich, *Russian Formalism: History—Doctrine* (The

Hague, 1955), pp. 9-10, 56-57, 149-50, where Erlich discusses the theories of Sklovskij, who was among the first to attack the simple idea of the image in poetry.

11. See the chapter on "Nature, Humanisme, Tragedie" in Alain Robbe-Grillet, *Pour un Nouveau Roman* (Paris, 1963).

12. The Polish poet Tadeusz Rózèwicz gives another example for the urgency of the problem of how to overcome metaphor, cf. *Rzecz poetycka* (Wydawnictwo Lódzkie, 1960).

13. Alfred Döblin, "Futuristische Worttechnik, Offener Brief an F. T. Marinetti," in *Der Sturm*, III (1913), 280.

14. Franz Kafka, *Tagebücher 1910-1923*, ed. Max Brod (New York and Frankfurt/M., 1951), p. 550.

15. *Ibid.*, p. 536.

16. Franz Kafka, "Beschreibung eines Kampfes," in *Gesammelte Werke*, ed. Max Brod (New York and Frankfurt/M., 1954), p. 42.

17. *Ibid.*

18. See the section "Bildformen" in Heinz Hillmann, *Franz Kafka: Dichtungstheorie und Dichtungsgestalt* (Bonn, 1964), pp. 136-47.

19. Franz Kafka, *Die Erzählungen*, ed. Klaus Wagenbach (Frankfurt/M., 1961).

20. E.g. Heinz Politzer, *Franz Kafka: Parable and Paradox* (New York, 1962). Cf. Hillmann, *op. cit.*, p. 165, note 112, where he discusses Politzer's term "parable."

21. Nelly Sachs, "In den Wohnungen des Todes," in *Gedichte der Nelly Sachs* (Frankfurt/M., 1961), p. 62.

22. It is serious poetry, most of all, that takes advantage of the paradox. Cf. Cleanth Brooks, "The Language of Paradox," in *Critiques and Essays on Criticism 1920-1948*, sel. R. W. Stallman (New York, 1949). Cf. also Harold Weinrich, "Semantik der kuhnen Metapher," *Deutsche Vierteljahrsschrift für Literaturwissenschaft und Geistesgeschichte*, XXXVII (1963), 325-44.

23. Paul Celan, *Der Meridian: Rede anlässlich der Verleihung des Georg-Büchner-Preises 1960* (Frankfurt/M., 1961), p. 19.

24. In Gustav René Hocke, *Manierismus in der Literatur: Sprach-Alchimie und esoterische Kombinationskunst* (Hamburg, 1959), p. 89.

25. Within the context of the passage from "Polifemo" (ll. 105-108) "red snow" is not at all an absurd metaphor of the type of Paul Eluard's "the earth is blue like an orange," as Hocke maintains (*ibid.*, p. 80). From the context it is quite clear how "red snow" is to be understood. Cf.

"Polifemo" (ll. 105-108) in Damaso Alonso, *Góngora y el 'Polifemo'* (Cuarta Edición, muy aumendata, Madrid, 1961), II, 12: "purpúreas rosas sobre Galatea la Alba entre lilos cándidos deshoja: duda el Amor cúal más su color sea, o púrpura nevada, o nieve roja." ("Aurora strews on Galatea petals plucked from purple roses and white lilies. Even Amor does not know what Galatea's color now is, whether it is snowy purple or red snow.")

26. Aristoteles, *Ars Poetica* 1457[b] 20. See also *Ars Rhetorica* 1407[a] 14.

27. This has caused Martin Heidegger to locate metaphor within the realm of metaphysics and not within the sphere of *"wesentliches Denken."* See Martin Heidegger, *Der Satz vom Grund* (Pfullingen, 1957), p. 89: "Mit der Einsicht in das Beschrankte der Metaphysik wird auch die massgebende Vorstellung von der 'Metapher' hinfallig. Sie gibt namlich das Ma fur unsere Vorstellung vom Wesen der Sprache. Darum dient die Metapher als vielgebrauchtes Hilfsmittel bei der Auslegung der Werke des Dichtens und des kunstlerischen Bildens uberhaupt. Das Metaphorische gibt es nur innerhalb der Metaphysik." The present attempt derives from my belief that it would be possible to develop another definition of metaphor than has been current so far and thus to abandon the metaphysical implications.

Beda Allemann is a native of Switzerland. He studied, mainly at Zurich, in the fields of Germanic languages, philosophy, and art. His doctorate at Zurich was directed by Emil Steiger, one of the foremost European scholars of Germanistic sciences. He has taught in Berlin, Paris, Leiden, and Kiel, and is now Professor of Modern German Literature at the University in Würzburg, Germany.

Owen Barfield was born in London in 1898. He went from Highgate School into the Royal Engineers (Signals) in the last years of World War I. He then continued his education and in 1921 was graduated from Wadham College, Oxford, with first-class honors in English Language and Literature. Subsequently he received the M.A., B.Litt., and B.C.L. degrees from that institution. He was a practicing solicitor at the English Bar in London from 1937 to 1959, when he retired. He is a fellow of the Royal Society of Literature and a member of International P.E.N., the Athenaeum Club, and the Anthroposophical Society in Great Britain. In 1964-65 he served as Visiting Professor of Philosophy and Letters at Drew University, Madison, New Jersey; and in 1965-66 he was appointed as a Visiting Professor at Brandeis University, Cambridge, Massachusetts.

Norman O. Brown was born in 1913 in El Oro, Mexico, where his father was active as a mining engineer. He was educated at Oxford University, the University of Chicago, and the University of Wisconsin, where he took his doctorate in 1942. Following a year as Professor of Languages at Nebraska Wesleyan University, he served three years as a research analyst with the Office of Strategic Services. He was Professor of Classics at Wesleyan University from 1946 to 1962. Currently he is a member of the faculty of the University of Rochester, where he is Wilson Professor of Classics and Comparative

Literature. He has been the recipient of awards from the Fund for the Advancement of Education of the Ford Foundation, the Guggenheim Foundation, and the Center for Advanced Study in the Behavioral Sciences.

Kenneth Burke was born in Pittsburgh, Pennsylvania, in 1897. He studied at Ohio State and Columbia Universities. He did research work with the Laura Spelman Rockefeller Memorial during 1926-27, and he was music critic of *The Dial* (1927-29) and *The Nation* (1934-36). Mr. Burke has lectured widely on the practice and theory of literary criticism, and he has taught that subject matter at the New School for Social Research, Bennington College, the University of Chicago, and Drew University. He has been the recipient of The Dial Award for distinguished service to American letters (1928), a Guggenheim Memorial Fellowship (1935), a grant from the American Academy of Arts and Letters, and a grant from the National Institute of Arts and Letters (1946); in 1963 he was elected to the American Academy of Arts and Sciences.

Julián Marías was born in Valladolid, Spain, in 1914. He studied under Ortega y Gassett at the University of Madrid in the early thirties and was cofounder, with Ortega, of the Institute of Humanities in 1948. In America he has taught at Wellesley, Harvard, Yale, University of California at Los Angeles, and in Spain he teaches American students from Middlebury College Graduate School and Mary Baldwin College. In 1964 he was awarded the first John F. Kennedy medal of the Institute of North American Studies in Barcelona, and in 1965 he received the highest honor bestowed on a Spanish writer: election to the Royal Spanish Academy. He is currently the director of the Seminar in Studies in Humanities in Madrid.

Heinrich Ott is a native of Switzerland. He was trained by the Theological Faculties of the University of Basel in Switzerland and the University of Marburg in Germany, and received the Doctorate of Theology degree from the former institution in 1955. He served as pastor at Castel, Graubunden, Switzerland (1952-57) and at Arisdorf, Basel-Laudslap (1957-62). He was a Privat Dozent in the

Theological Faculty at the University of Basel from 1956 to 1962, and since 1962 he has been Professor of Theology at that school. In addition, Professor Ott was Replacing Professor of Theology at the University of Bonn, Germany, during 1960-61, and Visiting Professor of Systematic Theology at the Graduate School of Drew University, Madison, New Jersey, during 1966.

Bibliography

THE FOLLOWING bibliographies of the contributors to this volume attempt to be complete through January, 1966, with the exception of the listings for Kenneth Burke and Julián Marías, which are selected. The major published bibliography for Kenneth Burke is found in: William H. Rueckert, *Kenneth Burke and the Drama of Human Relations* (Minneapolis: University of Minnesota Press, 1963). The complete writings of Julián Marías are in process of publication in his *Obras*, issued by Revista de Occidente, as indicated in the listing below.

BEDA ALLEMANN

Hölderlin und Heidegger. Zürich-Freiburg i. Br.: Atlantis Verlag, 1954. 2nd enlarged ed., 1956.
Hölderlins "Friedensfeier." Pfullingen: Neske, 1955.
Ironie und Dichtung. Friedrich Schlegel, Novalis, Solger, Kierke-gaard, Nietzsche, Thomas Mann, Musil. Pfullingen: Neske, 1956.
Ueber das Dichterische. Pfullingen: Neske, 1957.
"Le retournement natal dans l'oeuvre de Hölderlin," in *Aspects de la culture noire. Recherches et Débats. Centre Catholique des intellectuels français.* N.S., No. 24 (September, 1958). Paris: Librarie Arthème Fayard, 1958, pp. 183-99.
"Ironie" in W. KOHLSCHMIDT and W. MOHR, eds., *Reallexikon der deutschen Literaturgeschichte (begründet von P. Marker und W. Stammler)*, 2nd ed. (Berlin: De Gruyter, 1958), I, 756-61.

"Le symbole chez les pré-romantiques allemands," in *Le symbole. Recherches et Débats. Centre Catholique des intellectuels français.* N.S., No. 29 (December, 1959) (Paris: Librairie Arthème Fayard, 1959), pp. 112-19.

"Der Ort aber war die Wüste" in GÜNTHER NESKE, ed., *Martin Heidegger zum siebzigsten Geburtstag* (Pfullingen: Neske, 1959), pp. 204-216.

"Der Zwiespalt in der modernen Literatur," in *Glaube und Unglaube in unserer Zeit. Vier Zurcher Aulavorträge,* introduction by E. Staiger (Zürich: Atlantis Verlag, 1959), pp. 25-48.

"Gottfried Keller und das Skurrile," in *Jahresbericht der Gottfried-Keller-Gesellschaft 1959* (Zurich, 1960), pp. 1-16.

"Friedrich Dürrenmatt, Es steht geschrieben," in BENNO VON WIESE, ed., *Das deutsche Drama vom Barock bis zur Gegenwart. Interpretationen,* 2nd ed. (Düsseldorf: A. Bagel, 1960), II, 415-32.

Zeit und Figur beim späten Rilke. Ein Beitrag zur Poetik des modernen Gedichts. Pfullingen: Neske, 1961.

"Hinweis auf einen Gedicht-Raum," in *Nelly Sachs zu Ehren* (Frankfurt/M.: Suhrkamp, 1961), pp. 37-44.

"Rilke und Mallarmé. Entwicklung einer Grundfrage der symbolischen Poetik," in KARL RÜDIGER, ed., *Wort und Gestalt. Fünf Kapitel deutscher Dichtung* (München: Bayerischer Schulbuchverlag, 1962), pp. 81-100.

Gottfried Benn. Das Problem der Geschichte. Pfullingen: Neske, 1963. (*Opuscula aus Wissenschaft und Dichtung, 2.*)

"Dichter über Dichtung," in ADOLF FRISÉ, ed., *Definitionen. Essays zur Literatur* (Frankfurt/M.: Vittorio Klostermann, 1963), pp. 157-84.

"Experiment und Erfahrung in der Gegenwartsliteratur," in WALTER STROLZ, ed., *Experiment und Erfahrung in Wissenschaft und Kunst* (Freiburg i. Br. and München: K. Alber, 1963), pp. 266-96.

"Non-representational Modern German Poetry," in A. CLOSS, ed., *Reality and Creative Vision in German Lyrical Poetry* (London: Butterworth, 1963), pp. 71-79. Proceedings of the 15th Symposium of the Colston Research Society held in the University of Bristol, April 1-4, 1963.

"Ironie," in WOLF-HARTMUT FREIDRICH and WALTER KILLY, eds., *Das Fischer-Lexikon. Literature II* (Frankfurt/M.: Fischer Bücherei, 1963), 1, pp. 305-12.

"Franz Kafka: 'Der Prozess'," in BENNO VON WIESE, ed., *Der* deutsche Roman vom Barock bis zur Gegenwart. Struktur und Geschichte (Düsseldorf: A. Bagel, 1963), II, 234-90, 439-41.

"Paul Celan," in KLAUS NONNEMANN, ed., Deutsche Literatur der Gegenwart (Olten and Freiburg i. Br.: Walter, 1963), pp. 70-75.

"Kafka, Von den Gleichnissen," Zeitschrift für deutsche Philologie, LXXXIII, Sonderheft 3 (1964), 97-106.

OWEN BARFIELD

History in English Words. London: Faber and Faber, 1926. Faber paperback, 1962.

Poetic Diction: A Study in Meaning. London: Faber and Faber, 1929. New York: McGraw-Hill paperback, 1965.

Romanticism Comes of Age. London: Rudolf Steiner Press, 1944.

This Ever Diverse Pair (sub nom. G. A. L. BURGEON). London: Victor Gollancz, 1950.

Saving the Appearances: A Study in Idolatry. London: Faber and Faber, 1957. New York: Harcourt, Brace & World, paperback, 1965.

"The Meaning of the word 'Literal'," in L. C. KNIGHTS and BASIL COTTLE, eds., Metaphor and Symbol (London: Butterworth, 1960), pp. 48-63. Proceedings of the 12th Symposium of the Colston Research Society held in the University of Bristol, March 28-31, 1960.

"The Rediscovery of Meaning," Saturday Evening Post (January 7, 1961).

"Poetic Diction and Legal Fiction," in MAX BLACK, ed., The Importance of Language (Englewood Cliffs, N.J.: Prentice-Hall, Inc., 1962), pp. 51-71.

Worlds Apart (A Dialogue of the 1960's). London: Faber and Faber, 1963.

"The Riddle of the Sphinx," Arena (London: P.E.N. Centre for Writers in Exile). No. 29 (April, 1964), pp. 121-28. Paper prepared for the P.E.N. Congress, Oslo, Summer 1964.

Unancestral Voice. London: Faber and Faber, 1965.

"Introduction" to JOCELYN GIBB, ed., Light on C. S. Lewis (London: G. Bles, 1965; New York: Harcourt, Brace & World, 1966).

NORMAN O. BROWN

Hermes the Thief: The Evolution of a Myth. Madison, Wis.: University of Wisconsin Press, 1947.
Life Against Death. Middletown, Conn.: Wesleyan University Press, 1959. New York: Vintage paperback, 1959.
"Apocalypse: The Place of Mystery in the Life of the Mind," *Harper's Magazine,* CCXXII (May, 1961), 46-49.
Love's Body. New York: Random House, 1966.

KENNETH BURKE

The White Oxen and Other Stories. New York: Albert & Charles Boni, 1924.
Counter-Statement. New York: Harcourt, Brace & Co., 1931. Chicago: Phoenix paperback, 1957.
Towards a Better Life: Being a Series of Epistles or Declamations. New York: Harcourt, Brace & Co., 1932.
Permanence and Change: An Anatomy of Purpose. New York: New Republic, Inc., 1935.
"Symbolic War," *Southern Review,* II (1936-37), 134-47.
Attitudes Toward History. 2 vols. New York: New Republic, Inc., 1937. Boston: Beacon paperback, 1961.
"Surrealism," in JAMES LAUGHLIN, ed., *New Directions in Prose and Poetry* (Norfolk, Conn.: New Directions, 1940), pp. 563-79.
"Character of Our Culture," *Southern Review,* VI (1940-41), 675-94.
The Philosophy of Literary Form: Studies in Symbolic Action. Baton Rouge: Louisiana State University Press, 1941. New York: Vintage paperback, 1957.
"On Motivation in Yeats," *Southern Review,* VII (1941-42), 547-61.
"War and Cultural Life," *American Journal of Sociology,* XLVIII (1942-43), 404-10.
"The Tactics of Motivation," *Chimera,* I (Spring, 1943), 21-33; I (Summer, 1943), 37-53.
A Grammar of Motives. New York: Prentice-Hall, Inc., 1945. Cleveland: Meridian paperback (with *A Rhetoric of Motives*), 1962.
"Kinds of Criticism," *Poetry,* LXVIII (1946), 272-82.
"Ideology and Myth," *Accent,* VII (1947), 195-205.
A Rhetoric of Motives. New York: Prentice-Hall, Inc., 1950. Cleve-

land: Meridian paperback (with *A Grammar of Motives*), 1962.

"Vegetal Radicalism of Theodore Roethke," *Sewanee Review*, LVII (1950), 68-108.

"American Scholar Forum: The New Criticism," *American Scholar*, XX (1950-51), 86-104, 218-31.

"Rhetoric—Old and New," *The Journal of General Education*, V (1951), 202-209.

"Othello: An Essay to Illustrate a Method," *Hudson Review*, IV (1951), 165-203.

"Three Definitions," *Kenyon Review*, XII (1951), 173-92.

"Thanatopsis for Critics: A Brief Thesaurus of Deaths and Dyings," *Essays in Criticism*, II (1952), 369-75.

"Comments on Eighteen Poems by Howard Nemerov," *Sewanee Review*, LX (1952), 117-31.

"Form and Persecution in the Oresteia," *Sewanee Review*, LX (1952), 377-96.

"A 'Dramatistic' View of 'Imitation,'" *Accent*, XII (1952), 229-41.

"Ethan Brand: A Preparatory Investigation," *The Hopkins Review*, V (Winter, 1952), 45-65.

"Mysticism as a Solution to the Poets' Dilemma," STANLEY R. HOPPER, ed., *Spiritual Problems in Contemporary Literature* (New York: Harper & Bros., 1952), pp. 95-115. Published for The Institute for Religious and Social Studies.

"Postscripts on the Negative," *Quarterly Journal of Speech*, XXIX (1953), 209-16.

"Freedom and Authority in the Realm of the Poetic Imagination," in LYMAN BRYSON *et al.*, eds., *Freedom and Authority in Our Time: Twelfth Symposium of the Conference on Science, Philosophy, and Religion* (New York: Harper & Bros., 1953), pp. 365-75.

"A Dramatistic View of the Origins of Language," *Quarterly Journal of Speech*, XXXVIII (1952), 251-64, 446-60; XXXIX (1953), 79-92.

"Fact, Inference, and Proof in the Analysis of Literary Symbolism," in LYMAN BRYSON *et al.*, eds., *Symbols and Values: An Initial Study: Thirteenth Symposium of the Conference on Science, Philosophy, and Religion* (New York: Society for Science, Philosophy, and Religion, dist. by Harper & Bros., 1954), pp. 282-306.

"The Language of Poetry 'Dramatistically' Considered," *The Chi-*

cago Review, VIII (Fall, 1954), 88-102; IX (Spring, 1955), 40-72.

Book of Moments: Poems 1915-1954. Los Altos, Calif.: Hermes Publications, 1955.

"Policy Made Personal: Whitman's Verse and Prose—Salient Traits," in MILTON HINDUS, ed., *Leaves of Grass One Hundred Years After* (Stanford: Stanford University Press, 1955), pp. 74-108.

"Linguistic Approach to Problems of Education," in NELSON B. HENRY, ed., *Modern Philosophies and Education: The Fifty-fourth Year Book of the National Society for the Study of Education* (Chicago: University of Chicago Press, 1955), LIV, Part I, 259-303.

"Symbol and Association," *Hudson Review*, IX (1956-57), 212-25.

"Towards a Total Conformity: A Metaphysical Fantasy," *The Literary Review*, II (1957-58), 203-207.

"The Poetic Motive," *Hudson Review*, XI (1958), 54-63.

"Towards a Post-Kantian Verbal Music," *Kenyon Review*, XX (1958), 529-46.

"On Catharsis, or Resolution," *Kenyon Review*, XXI (1959), 337-75.

"Myth, Poetry and Philosophy," *Journal of American Folklore*, LXXII (1959), 283-306.

"Motion, Action, Words," *Teachers College Record*, LXII (1960), 244-49.

"The Brain Beautiful," *Bennington College Bulletin*, XXIX (November, 1960), 4-7.

The Rhetoric of Religion: Studies in Logology. Boston: Beacon Press, 1961.

"Catharsis—Second View," *Centennial Review*, V (1961), 107-32.

"What Are the Signs of What? A Theory of 'Entitlement,'" *Anthropological Linguistics*, IV (June, 1962), 1-23.

"The Thinking of the Body: Comments on the Imagery of Catharsis in Literature," *The Psychoanalytic Review*, L (Fall, 1963), 25-68.

"Definition of Man," *Hudson Review*, XVI (Winter, 1963-64), pp. 491-514.

"Art—and the First Rough Draft of Living," *Modern Age*, VIII (Spring, 1964), pp. 155-65.

"Shakespearean Persuasion," *The Antioch Review*, XXIV (Spring, 1964), 19-36.

"The Unburned Bridges of Poetics, or, How Keep Poetry Pure?" *Centennial Review*, VIII (Fall, 1964), 391-97.

"Faust II—The Ideas Behind the Imagery," *Centennial Review*, IX (Fall, 1965), 367-97.

JULIÁN AGUILERA MARÍAS

Don Quixote as Seen by Sancho Panza. Basavangudi: Bangalore, 1956.

Reason and Life: The Introduction to Philosophy. Trans. by KEN-NETH S. REID and EDWARD SARMIENTO. New Haven: Yale University Press, 1956. London: Hollis & Carter, 1956.

Ataraxía y alcionisimo. Madrid: Instituto Ibys, 1957.

Obras: Tomo I ("Historia de la filosofía"). Madrid: Editorial Revista de Occidente, 1958.

Obras: Tomo II ("Introducción a la filosofía"). Madrid: Editorial Revista de Occidente, 1958.

El lugar del peligro. Madrid: Taurus, 1958.

Obras: Tomo III ("Aquí y ahora," "Ensayos de convivencia," "Los Estados Unidos en escorzo"). Madrid: Editorial Revista de Occidente, 1959.

Obras: Tomo IV ("San Anselmo y el insensato," "La filosofía del Padre Gratry," "Ensayos de teoría," "El intelectual y su mundo"). Madrid: Editorial Revista de Occidente, 1959.

Obras: Tomo V ("Miguel de Unamuno," "La escuela de Madrid," "La imagen de la vida humana"). Madrid: Editorial Revista de Occidente, 1960.

Ortega I: Circumstancia y vocación. Madrid: Editorial Revista de Occidente, 1960.

El tema de hombre. Madrid: Espasa-Calpe, 1960.

Experienca de la vida. Madrid: Editorial Revista de Occidente, 1960.

Obras: Tomo VI ("El método historico de las generaciones," "La estructura social," "El oficio del pensamiento"). Madrid: Editorial Revista de Occidente, 1961.

Ortega ante Goethe. Madrid: Taurus, 1961.

Imagen de la India. Madrid: Editorial Revista de Occidente, 1961.

"Introduction and Notes" to José Ortega y Gasset, *Meditations on Quixote*. Trans. by EVELYN RUGG and DIEGO MARÍN. New York: W. W. Norton & Co., Inc., 1961.

Los Españoles. Madrid: Editorial Revista de Occidente, 1962.

History of Philosophy. New York: Dover Publications, 1963.

Modos de vivir: Un observador español en los Estados Unidos. Ed. EDWARD R. MULVIHILL and ROBERTO G. SÁNCHEZ. New York: Oxford University Press, 1964.

HEINRICH OTT

"Neuere Publikationen zum Problem von Geschichte und Geschichtlichkeit," *Theologische Rundschau,* Neue Folge, XXI (1953), 63-96.
"Objektivierendes und existentiales Denken," *Theologische Zeitschrift* (Basel), X (1954), 257-89. "Objectification and Existentialism," in H. W. BARTSCH, ed., *Kerygma and Myth,* II. London: S.P.C.K., 1962, pp. 306-335.
Geschichte und Heilsgeschichte in der Theologie Rudolf Bultmanns. (Beiträge zur Historischen Theologie, vol. XIX.) Tübingen: Mohr, 1955.
Review of F. Buri, *Theologie der Existenz. Theologische Zeitschrift* (Basel), XI (1955), 71-75.
"Existentiale Interpretation als Problem der christlichen Predigt," *Theologische Zeitschrift* (Basel), XI (1955), 115-27.
"Die sachgemässe Auslegung der Heiligen Schrift," *Reformatio* Zürich–Frankfurt/M.: Gotthelf-Verlag, 1956.
Verkündigung und Existenz. Gedanken zur Lehre von der Predigt. Zürich–Frankfurt/M.: Gotthelf-Verlag, 1956.
"Der Gedanke der Souveränität Gottes in der Theologie Karl Barths." (Festgabe für Karl Barth zum siebzigsten Geburtstag, Teil II.) *Theologische Zeitschrift* (Basel), XII (1956), 409-24.
"Anselms Versöhnungslehre," *Theologische Zeitschrift* (Basel), XIII (1957), 183-99.
Eschatologie. Versuch eines dogmatischen Grundrisses. (Theologische Studien, Heft 53.) Zürich and Zollikon: Evangelischer Verlag Zollikon, 1958.
"Entmythologisierung," in K. GALLING, ed., *Die Religion in Geschichte und Gegenwart* (3rd ed.), (Tübingen: Mohr, 1958), II, cols. 495-99.
Review of Friedrich Gogarten, *Verhängnis und Hoffnung der Neuzeit. Theologische Zeitschrift* (Basel), XIV (1958), 68-69.
"Theologie als Gebet und als Wissenschaft," *Theologische Zeitschrift* (Basel), XIV (1958), 120-32.
Denken und Sein. Der Weg Martin Heideggers und der Weg der

Theologie. Zürich and Zollikon: Evangelischer Verlag Zollikon, 1959.

"Heilsgeschichte"; "Kerygma," in K. GALLING, ed., *Die Religion in Geschichte und Gegenwart* (3rd ed.), (Tübingen: Mohr, 1959), III, cols. 187-89, 1250-54.

"Römer 1, 19ff. als dogmatisches Problem," *Theologische Zeitschrift* (Basel), XV (1959), 40-50.

Die Frage nach dem historischen Jesus und die Ontologie der Geschichte. (Theologische Studien, Heft 62.) Zürich and Zollikon: Evangelischer Verlag Zollikon, 1960. "The Historical Jesus and the Ontology of History," in C. E. BRAATEN and ROY A. HARRISVILLE, eds., *The Historical Jesus and the Kerygmatic Christ* (New York–Nashville: Abingdon, 1964), pp. 142-71.

Dogmatik und Verkündigung. Zürich and Zollikon: Evangelischer Verlag Zollikon, 1961.

"Was ist systematische Theologie?" *Zeitschrift für Theologie und Kirche. Beiheft 2* (September, 1961), pp. 19-46. "What is Systematic Theology?" in JAMES M. ROBINSON and JOHN B. COBB, JR., eds., *The Later Heidegger and Theology.* (New Frontiers in Theology, Vol. I.) New York: Harper & Row, 1963, pp. 77-111.

"Linguaggio e Comprensione," in *Demitizzazione e Imagine. Archivio di Filosofia* (Organo dell' Istituto di Studi Filosofici, Università di Romà). Padova: Cedam, 1962, Nos. 1-2, pp. 81-91.

Glaube und Bekennen. Ein Beitrag zum ökumenischen Dialog. (Begegnung: Eine ökumenische Schriftenreihe, Band II.) Basel: Friedrich Reinhardt, 1963.

Die Lehre des I. Vatikanischen Konzils. Ein evangelischer Kommentar. (Begegnung: Eine ökumenische Schriftenreihe, Band IV.) Basel: Friedrich Reinhardt, 1963.

"Response to the American Discussion," in JAMES M. ROBINSON and JOHN B. COBB, JR., eds., *The Later Heidegger and Theology.* (New Frontiers in Theology, Vol. I.) New York: Harper & Row, 1963, pp. 198-212.

"Hermeneutique et Eschatologie," in *Archivio di Filosofia* (Organo dell' Istituto di Studi Filosofici, Università di Romà). Padova: Cedam, 1963, Nos. 1-2, pp. 105*ff*.

Review of Fritz Buri, *Christliche Dogmatik. Basler Nachrichten,* No. 421 (October 6, 1963).

"Existentiale Interpretation und anonyme Christlichkeit," in ERICH DINKLER, ed., *Zeit und Geschichte* (Dankesgabe an Rudolf Bultmann zum achtzigsten Geburtstag.) (Tübingen: Mohr, 1964), pp. 367-79.

"Was ist Wirklichkeit?" *Deutsches Pfarrerblatt*, LXIV (1964), 369-73.

"Das Problem des nicht-objektivierenden Denkens und Redens in der Theologie," *Zeitschrift für Theologie und Kirche*, LXI (1964), 327-52. "The Problem of Nonobjectifying Thinking and Speaking in Theology" in *Journal for Theology and the Church*, III (1966).